History Of Mechanicsburg, Ohio

Joseph Ware

HISTORY

of

MECHANICSBURG, OHIO

BY

JOSEPH WARE, M. A., Lit. D.

COLUMBUS, OHIO:
THE F. J. HEER PRINTING CO.
1917

CONTENTS.

MECHANICSBURG.

MECHANICSBURG is a long and cumbersome word, but the name has its origin in a beautiful and poetic legend, the love of Wawanita, an Indian maiden.

The story which is here recorded for the first time gives a romantic interest to the awkward name and forms a basis for the details of its origin. In order to have a proper setting for the romance, the mind must be divested of the thought of the present, the beautiful shaded streets, handsome residences, velvety lawns, business houses, public buildings, and the imagination must clothe the great State of Ohio again with the primeval forest, the home of the bear, the timber wolf, the deer and the wild turkey. This particular section was not different in this respect, and was the common hunting ground of nomadic tribes of Red Men.

A clear, cool stream, called by the Indians "Dabra,"* divided two long sloping hills covered with a tangled undergrowth of immense wild grape vines. Its pure waters originated in a very large spring about a mile above. Its borders were fringed with beautiful old willows. On the hillside sloping Northward could be seen among the trees the wigwams of an Indian village, of the Shawnee tribe. The largest, built of bark set on end, the smoke issuing from an opening in the top, was that of the great chief, Ohito. Standing in front of it could be seen his beautiful daughter, Wawanita (Face in the water). She was fairer and more gentle than her dark-skinned, coarse-haired, rough-featured people. She was as natural in her loveliness as the uncultivated wild rose. Yet in her face and manner there was a droop of sadness. As was natural her beauty and position had not failed to attract the attention of the young braves. The most persistent was Sugumo (Loud

---

* The Indian name "Dabra" meaning "clear water," was afterward corrupted by white men into "Darby."

Thunder). Because he was strong and fleet, he almost demanded her of Ohito, her father, offering to give him many scalps of his enemies, and to provide him venison and bear meat in abundance. Ohito hesitated, Sugumo was like a dark cloud, while she was the bright sunbeam of his wigwam. Sugumo would treat her no better than he would his dogs. The father also knew that she did not love him. He could see that she was afraid, that she was troubled. There was one thing about her that he did not know, which was that she cherished vaguely in her inmost soul the vision of an ideal companion, not knowing whether or not she would ever realize the object of her longing. In this she had no confidant except an old and gnarled willow tree, which cast a soft green shadow in the placid waters of the Dabra. Hidden here she would sit for hours whispering the secrets of her inmost soul, as to a sympathizing friend. The old willow let her branches hang lower and her green leaves would whisper in the breeze, "Shelee, savee, shelee" (wait and see) and she would answer, "Patient old willow, how *can* I wait?" She only heard the repeated answer, "Shelee" (wait). The gnarled old willow listened patiently to her one little plaint repeated over and over as the bird sings over and over its plaintive melody,

"Shawanee Wawanita,
Ohi, Hi, totem
Siwanee Wa, wa."

The brook ran still under the willow boughs, listening to her heartbreak. The image in the water of her lovely face resembled the image pictured in her mind. That she knew of no such person increased her longing. The rough features of Sugumo only caused terror. The other maidens of the tribe with heavy features and coarse hair could love him for the enemies he scalped and the meat he provided. Would the willow tree not ask the Great Spirit to turn his thoughts toward them? So she would plead until the great sun had set and the woods were filled with darkness. And the wolves were gathering, howling their hunger, when she would slip away to her father's wigwam on the side hill.

One beautiful day in June as she sat under the old familiar tree, strange sounds burst on the ancient solitudes. Mingled with the shrill shrieking fifes was the thump of great drums, or tom toms, and many strange voices not far away. Startled, she sprang to her feet and parting the vines crept noiselessly until she saw the cause of the strange commotion, a motley company of citizen soldiers carrying on their shoulders heavy flintlock muskets. Nearest to her a youth of manly beauty was watching a compass which he held in his hand. He was the chief mechanic of the expedition. Right in her sight at last was her soul ideal. In her native simplicity she would have run to embrace him, had not her modesty held her back. After the men had been directed where to pitch their tents, he lifted his eyes and was startled to see a vision of aboriginal loveliness, that quickened his heart beats. For a moment he stood and gazed, fearing that an advance would frighten the vision away. He then with hands crossed upon his breast advanced slowly, saying, "Captain Culver." The fair lips parted and in musical tones he heard, "Wawanita, Shawnee." They exchanged smiles of the same meaning in all languages. Repeating, "Siwanee Wa, Wa! Siwanee Wa, Wa!", she artlessly stepped forward to meet him. Conversation could go no farther except by signs, in which love soon found a way. When the sun was in the West he was to come to the willow tree on the bank of the stream. He motioned, "Would there be treachery?" A quick tear in her eye and her extended hand gave him a shamed assurance. It was not love at first sight with her, it was but the realization of her long time ideal. The reluctance of parting when she entered again into the unknown forest showed how much his heart was already involved. She stopped on her way to tell the old willow the glad news, "Siwanee Wa, Wa!"

Captain Culver had gained the information that there was a large Shawnee village on the opposite hillside. Thereupon General Hull decided that they would build a circular fort, the breastworks of earth to be crowned with a stockade.*

While the fort was building many happy hours were spent by Captain Culver and Wawanita under the old willow tree. He found that her name meant "face in the water." He greatly enjoyed learning their picture language. She learned the harsh English because she loved her teacher. "Mechanic — this?"

---

* Few are aware that the earthworks of this fort situated just below the house of the late Milton Cheney, were shoulder high even as late as 1850.

she would inquire. "This, water?" "This, face?" "This?" Then she walked away and came back. "Went away and came back." He knew what she meant by this. He would point his finger, "Now, say them." And she did, and he would praise her. "Wawanita speak good. This is a kiss." Her laugh was like rippling water. How is it known that heaven is love? It is that the happiness of two innocent souls in their association is the greatest bliss known on earth.

The next morning after the fort was completed General Hull ordered Culver to his tent for a private conference. After saluting, the General motioned Culver to be seated beside him.

"Captain Culver, as you know, this fort is completed. I suppose you are sorry for it." Smiling at his confusion, "There must be no further delay. Tomorrow the expedition goes forward. As a loyal soldier you will be ready. Have the axes sharp and the powder dry. I do not like certain movements of the Indians."

"General Hull, every thing shall be in readiness." "My soldiers tell me that you meet your little Indian girl every evening outside the fort. Beware, the Indian nature is treacherous." "Not hers." "The danger lies in overconfidence. She may have an Indian lover. You doubtless know what jealousy is. You might take her with you, but it would arouse the Indians and make them still more dangerous. They are already disposed to join the British against us." "General, I do not think it would be best. This war will not last very long. We whipped the British once and can do it again. She will await my return."

"Very well, bid her goodbye this evening. Wait! Take the best musket in the command with you. See that the powder is dry. Captain, we can not spare you in this stage of the game. Take no chances. Exactly at sunrise we leave here and take a straight course for Fort Urbana."

"General, my wise little Indian says that there is a deep marshy lake just over the hill and that the Indians will ambush us there. She says for us to turn toward the sunset when we get to the top of the hill."

"Can we trust her?"

"I am sure we can."

"Very well. We will keep the muskets close to the axemen. Come back early tonight."

"I will do as you command, General."

All that fateful evening Wawanita felt that something was wrong and that she was about to lose the idol of her heart. After a long silence she half sobbed, "Mechanic go away?" "Yes, but Mechanic come back." After another long silence the quick ear of Wawanita caught the sound of a breaking twig. Springing to her feet, she handed Culver his gun. Catching sight of a long white arrow thrust through the bushes she pulled him behind the great willow just as the well-aimed arrow whizzed by. Wawanita took Culver's cocked hat and held it out on a stick. An arrow pierced it through and fell in the water beyond. She let the hat fall as though it were a person. Knowing the Indian nature well enough to know that he would want to kill Culver himself and had therefore brought no one with him, risking her life, she peeped. Sugumo it was, rushing madly through the brush to scalp his victim. "Shoot, quick! Shoot, quick!" Culver took good aim and fired. The old musket did not fail him. Sugumo fell forward in the weeds and brush.

"Mechanic go. Mechanic come back someday. Wawanita wait. Mechanic run. Warriors hear gun." He delayed only long enough to take an ardent kiss and shouted back, "Wawanita wait. Mechanic come back."

At the break of day, the citizen army of General Hull filed out of the fort, following the axemen, who immediately began to blaze the trail. Captain Culver, the chief mechanic was leading the way with his compass in one hand and his musket in the other. Just as he came to the brook, he swerved slightly in order to pass near the willow tree. The beautiful "face in the water" was not there. With a deep sigh, almost a heart break, he crossed over and proceeded up the opposite hill on which was the Shawnee village. Its size was surprising even to a woodsman. As they passed through the one wide path,* Wawanita was standing in front of her father's wigwam. She was as immovable as a statue. She gave no sign of recognition. She dare show none. At the top of the hill the column turned

---

* The Main street of Mechanicsburg as it was afterwards laid off in 1814.

due west toward Fort Urbana, thus avoiding the marsh ground above the lake.

Our history has no further concern with General Hull's military expedition except that when the army was disgracefully surrendered to a mere handful of British at Detroit, Captain Culver, with John Kane, escaping into the wilderness, followed the well known trail with persevering labor, much privation and hardship back to the spot where Culver hoped, although with some misgiving, to meet again his beloved Indian girl.

I can not describe the grief and horror that overcame him as he eagerly descended the hill slope to find the Indian village gone, he knew not where. Nothing was left behind, even the ashes of their fires were scattered. Running here and there he could discover no marks of their going. The wild, wide wilderness held in its bosom the secret. In the frenzy of his passionate grief he would cry aloud her name, "Wawanita! Wawanita!" The eternal silence only mocked his wail. He ran down to the willow tree. Hanging to the arrow, still imbedded in its trunk, was the plain gold ring that he had given her. Conjecture set him wild. Did she regard their separation as hopeless? Did it mean that she had given him up? Torn with conflicting thoughts, his mind wandered. He would sit all day looking into the bright waters of the brook. Good old kind Nature tried to relieve him. He would imagine that he saw her beautiful face reflected in the stream. Perhaps the illusion saved him. He might always see it there, proving that he was hopelessly demented. He would talk as though she were sitting on the bank beside him. The obsession would be permanent. He was fast settling into the mania of despair.

On a beautiful Indian summer evening the big red sun was in the West, the beautiful face of Wawanita really did appear in the silver waters. She was really sitting beside him. The expression varied just a little. "Mechanic waited. Wawanita come back." Her love had indeed been true. She had wandered alone through the trackless wilderness to find her only love. He was no longer insane. He had met the only cure. The very first thing he did was to place the golden band on her slender finger again and press it to his lips. The scenes of their reunion can be filled in by the imagination. They can not be described. Just as the golden sun was setting he took

her by the hand and led her across the brook and up the trail
even to the top of the hill where he had built for Kane a double
log cabin.* As they entered, Culver said, "John, I was right.
I saw her face in the water. We want to get married." "But
there is no Squire or Minister." "John, you will do. Just say,
'whom God hath joined together, let no man put asunder.'
That is enough." "Well, so be it then. I will pronounce you
man and wife." No priestly ceremony was ever more binding
than this simple one of the wilderness cabin.

Culver with his army compass laid off a town for Kane
on the immediate site of the Shawnee village of Ohito. Kane
and Culver were discussing a name for it. Wawanita was
called in to suggest a name. She at once said "MECHANIC,"
her first and dearest English word. They at once added
"BURG", and this is the picturesque origin of the name of our
beautiful town.

CHAPTER 2.

In the Beginning.

THE original town plat of Mechanicsburg was laid off in
unbroken forest by John Kain. It had 28 inlots, each
7 rods or 115½ feet square, fronting on the two streets,
Sandusky and Chillicothe (now Main), with 11-foot alleys back
of them.

It had 16 outlots, each 10½ rods square, making the whole
plat 1,012 feet square, containing 23½ acres. The land on
which it was laid was in the Virginia Military survey number
4747, patented to William Reynolds, who transferred it to
Robert Means, he to Duncan McArthur. When it came into
the possession of John Kain, he laid out the streets 66 feet
wide and the alleys 11 feet. Why they were made so narrow
cannot be conjectured as the land was very slow of sale at
$1.00 per acre. Kain sold some of the most eligible lots at
from one to five dollars each, the remainder he gave away.

---

* Major John C. Baker tore it away when he built a fine residence
on the site. It is now the site of the home of Darius J. Burnham at
the head of Main street. The old oak tree which stood in front of the
cabin is still standing there in 1917.

As to its geographical location, it is situated in the State of Ohio, Champaign County, Goshen Township.

The original or beginning corner is the Southwest corner of the public square. It was the center stake of Ohita's wigwam. In excavating for the foundation of the present Anderson Inn an inscribed brick monument was found buried there, and the watertable of the Inn was set immediately over it. The watertable at this time was made a bench mark for the town, being 47½ feet above low water mark of Darby Creek. The entire ascent of Main street being 140 feet. On the top of the hill John Kain built a large log house near where Darius J. Brunham now lives. Major J. C. Baker tore the house away in recent years. A very old oak tree still stands as a witness of the original forest. This was the first house built inside of the present corporation.

The first cabin erected in the original plat was on lot number eleven where Boulton and Ware's store now stands. John Owen cleared a space in the timber and built the little log store room. Into this he put a stock of general merchandise and also started what he entitled, "The Mechanicsburg Bank." The sides and ends of this store and bank were built of undressed logs, the bark still on them. The crevices between them were chinked with split pieces, these were daubed with mud to exclude rain and wind. The joist and rafters were poles. The floor was of puncheon, that is, long poles split and laid with the plain side up. What a contrast to the smooth hardwood floors of our time! The roof of split clapboards was held in place by other cross poles. There was no attempt at plastering. The large outside chimney was made of sticks daubed with clay, thickly coated on the inside. The one small window in lieu of glass had greased cloth. A solid heavy shutter was securely fastened in this aperture at night. The door was of heavy material dressed with an axe. It was hung with wooden hinges turning on a round stick, and locked with an iron bar and padlock. The supports for the shelving in this primitive store and bank were wooden pins driven into holes made with a podauger. Here this man of enterprise sold what little he did sell at an enormous profit. Calico, which would fade, and most of it would at this time, he sold at 25 cents a yard, coarse salt at four dollars per bushel, a paper of homemade pins fifty cents.

Whilst what the settlers had to exchange brought very little, eggs five cents per dozen, butter six and a quarter cents per pound, chickens ten and twelve cents each. Horses were $15 to $25, cattle $10 to $15 per head. It is no wonder the settlers made their own clothing fastening them together with pins instead of buttons, and lived on what the ground, which was generous, produced.

John Owen was president of the first bank run in connection with his store, and Samuel R. Miller was the cashier. It is rumored that the storage vault for the bank's money was a woman's stocking. The Mechanicsburg Bank, according to the custom of the times, issued small currency notes, called shin-plasters. But alas! a fellow got into his possession sixty dollars of this currency and presented it for redemption. Such a run as this on the stocking caused the bank to suspend. It became defunct.

The second building in the village was a log tavern, built after the fashion of the store. It stood on the corner of the public square, not number 11. This site has been used as a a tavern, hotel or inn from that time until now. The first landlord was Warret Owen, the second was George Warren, then William Kelly.

It was not long until many cabins, with their smoking chimneys, in small clearings showed that the village was growing. The streets also were gradually being cleared. Some of the very worst places in them were PAVED with what was called "Corduroy", that is small round poles were thrown close together across the street. A forcible illustration of their condition at that time is given in the following incident.

Colonel Thomas Moore moved here from Kentucky in an ox wagon. As he came down Main street to a point just above the public square, the oxen mired down and one of them died before it could be gotten out. Our William Moore distinctly remembered this incident, although he was but four years old. Main street was no more than a miry track through the dogfennel. Walking in the timber was better than on this public thoroughfare.

Every improved lot had to be fenced on account of the hogs and all other stock running at large. The writer has a vision of a great drove of large white hogs running, squealing, up West Sandusky street at the loud call of Uncle Charlie Joyner.

The pioneer life had its privations and limitations, its toils and hardships but in the isolation of early days there is compensation, friendship and companionship are increased rather than diminished. There may be extreme lonesomeness in a populous city but there is an intimate acquaintanceship in the sparse settlement. Even the sight of the smoke ascending from a neighboring cabin chimney is a social pleasure. Every individual knows the affairs of all, either of business or household concerns, or what young man keeps company with what girl. All the intimacies as well as animosities are common property.

As late as 1830 the census gave Mechanicsburg only 98 white inhabitants and one colored. These eighteen or nineteen families were almost completely shut in to each other. The few scattering settlers about completed their world.

CHAPTER 3.

Early Business Enterprises.

THE water power which Little Darby furnished as it descended to the level country to the eastward was the origin and source of future progress of the town. Andrew Staley, a young millwright, came here and built a small log grist mill west of Main street. The neighbors and settlers donated the labor of themselves and teams to construct the race and mill pond. Afterward the race was continued across Main street and a much larger frame mill with saw mill attached was erected on the present site. The great overshot wheel as it was turned by the water pouring over it and dashing in foam down the tail race to join the creek again was a constant source of wonder to the children. The vacant space above and in front of the mill was often crowded with wagons, some of them coming twenty miles to have their grists ground. Many of these had to remain over night awaiting their turns. The scene at night was worthy of a Homer's song. The campfire light reflected from the faces of the men, the great white covered wagons, the crunching horses, the silent stars looking down upon them, the constant whirr of the mill, the passing in and out of the dusty miller, Andy Staley, busy but mild, sweet-tempered and patient made a scene long to be remembered.

A grist mill and saw mill was built one half mile up the creek in 1823 by Jonathon Cheney, then owned by Jacob Hazel, then by Rich, Hart & Good. Afterward it was known as the Hunter and Johnson mill.

Jonathon Cheney, Jr. then used the water to operate a carding machine. Owen and Dye had a woolen factory below town afterward operated by Stewart and Mickle.

The first tan yard was located by Colonel Moore on the swift running Clover Run, near the present Maple Grove Cemetery, afterward moving it to the outlot back of Inlot No. 6, just back of the Henry Cheney property on West Sandusky street. Chapman and Jones had a tannery on the race above the mill pond. This was later operated by Henry and William Moore.

There was an ashery on the Darby near where it crosses Main street opposite the Staley Mill. An ashery was a place where the farmers brought ashes from their immense fireplaces and clearings, to be leached and made into soda and cream of tartar. This by-product was the source of considerable revenue.

There were other less pretentious enterprises. Colonel Jesse S. Bates had a carding machine run by tread power, using an ox for the purpose.

Nick Wynant, a harmlessly insane man, used a large black bear to turn his lathe.

Hupp and Newcomb had a cabinet shop with an undertaking department, making by hand furniture and also coffins. They took the measure of the corpse by notches on a stick if they had no rule with them. The undertakers' charge was $1.00 per foot. Thus for a person five feet in height the bill would be $5.00. The coffins were very plain affairs, made of wild cherry and black walnut. A small hearse with glass in the sides was the wonder of the community.

Another enterprise was a hat shop of Uncle Charlie Joyner on lot No. 9 on the south side of West Sandusky street. Some mischievous young men broke in one night and weighed one of the hats and it weighed four pounds. They were stiff hats made of wool and fur picked and matted together and moulded on a block.

Willis Horr, shortly after matches were invented, started a match factory on lot No. 3 on the north side of East Sandusky street. They were very crude affairs. Sometimes with hard rubbing they would light, sometimes they would not. If they did, they would almost suffocate one with sulphur fumes. He made them entirely by hand, sawed out and split the blocks of pine, and hired girls to dip the ends in sulphur.

Southeast of town there were two small distilleries, making good the saying of Job, "and Satan came also among them." Their products were not quite so injurious on account of their proximity to large springs of water.

Coming under the category of manufactories are the boot and shoe shops of those days. The boots and shoes were made by hand from very heavy cowhide leather, the thick heavy soles being nailed and pegged on. Morocco slippers were out of the question. At the dances the heavy footwear made the cabins shake.

Another productive industry was the tailor shop. Here the homespun cloth was made into clothing by the cross-legged tailor. Such men was Adam Woods, James Carlton, and T. J. Glendenning.

The saddles and harness were all made by hand. J. L. ("Dad") Magruder was one of the first in this line.

The millinery business might also be classed as a factory. The women's bonners were usually made of leghorn. Every few years instead of buying a new one the old bonnet was made over by the milliner. The process was to rip it up, rebraid it, plaster it with sulphur, suspend it in a barrel over burning sulphur to whiten it, then wash it in suds of home-made soap, and while still damp, place it over a wooden block and iron it. It was then ready to be retrimmed with ribbon.

At an early day a log tavern was built by Theoderick Spain on the corner across the alley North of the Magruder building, where Gilbert's store and Jobe's bakery burned in 1916. Spain was the first postmaster. There was no civil service in those days and he and his descendants held the office for thirty years. The postoffice was off the alley in the rear of the tavern. When you had hunted him up, he was accommodating enough to unlock the door and go in and get you a letter, if there was any. The letters were sealed with red sealing wax, the postage on them was twenty-five cents. This tavern was afterward called the Wahoo House. It was the point where the four-horse stage coach, carrying the mail from West Jefferson stopped on its road to Urbana. As the driver, Sam Brown, came in sight of the town, he would blow his horn, crack his whip and come up at breakneck speed, breaking the stillness of the solitude, causing a flutter of excitement especially among the small boys, who looked upon the driver as a heroic figure.

David L. Tullis was one of the first blacksmiths. His shop was where the Richard Williams residence stands.

Among the early doctors were Doctors Fiffin, Lawler, Ebeneezer Cheney, Obed Horr, Ebeneezer Owen and Colliver.

The oldest landmark still standing on its original site is the building just South of the Masonic Temple, now Venrick's Tin Shop. The sign painted on the front of it, "Owen and Keyes, Drug Store" is still there, though somewhat dimmed by the last coat of paint put over it. One of the proprietors was the father of Warren Keyes. The principal drugs were calomel, quinine and tar.

Perhaps the most notable building of the early days was what was called "Long Ornery", a long, narrow, one-story building fronting on the public square and extending North on Main street. Jesse S. Bates had a general store in the front and his dwelling in the back. Other early storekeepers were French Rambo, Obed Horr, McCorkle and Ware, Joseph C. Brand.

As usual the places of trade were also the social centers, the loafing places for the men, where various questions were discussed, news disseminated and jokes told. In all of which the proprietor had ample time to join, unless it was the tavern-keeper on general muster days and especially on circus days. Hiram Gutridge, the son-in-law of Uncle Charlie Joyner, on circus days would run from the large barn to the tavern inquiring vociferously, "Where's Pap, where's Pap?" Every boy in town got up before daylight and went out to meet the elephants. Settlers for miles around would come in wagons, on horseback, and on foot.

Muster days were also times of considerable excitement. All men of a certain age were compelled to drill. Some through drunkenness, others through lack of interest could never keep step. The expedient was tried of tying hay on the right foot and straw on the left and as they marched the captain would keep time by shouting, "Hay foot! Straw foot!"

The officers felt the dignity and insisted on the muster. The men broke it up by electing to office the most disreputable men they could find, such as Aaron Devers, Colonel, and Sol Valentine, Captain.

CHAPTER 4.

The Early Church.

THE great social as well as religious center was the church. The government of the Methodist Episcopal church with its strong centralized power was the efficient agency in sending the traveling itinerant into the almost trackless wilderness, preaching in the settlers' cabins or wherever opportunity, however humble, offered. It is astonishing to know that this circuit extended from Sandusky on Lake Erie to the Ohio river. The preachers would pass and repass every two weeks, preaching in the cabins week nights and Sundays. Through peril and exposure they traveled on horseback, with a change of clothing, a Bible and hymn book in a leather saddle bag. They were not sleek feather-bed divines but bronzed and hardy pioneers.

Their sermons made up in unction and length what they lacked in polish. The usual length was two hours and their delivery loud and vociferous, and yet the people sitting on hard seats without backs would listen attentively until the close, when the preacher as well as the subject would be exhausted.

The first preaching place and school house was erected in 1814. It was built of logs unhewn except on the inside, made a little more presentable by dressing them some with the axe. It was at first warmed by a kettle of coals. I gather this from the story that is told of Aunt Katie Millice. When she shouted she had a fashion of tripping forward and backward. In the latter movement she accidently sat down in the kettle of live coals, thereby increasing the excitement if not the religious fervor. A gravel hill on the east side of the corporation was deeded to the church by Andrew Staley for a graveyard.

The following is the roll of members of the church at this time: Mr. and Mrs. William Wood, Mr. and Mrs. Thomas Lansdale, Mr. and Mrs. Michael Conn, Mr. and Mrs. Richard Lansdale, Mr. and Mrs. Henry Millice, Mr. and Mrs. John Wynant, Mr. and Mrs. Christopher Millice, Mr. and Mrs. Philip Wynant, Mr. and Mrs. Alexander McCorkle.

In 1819 a hewed frame church was built a little east of the old log one, nearer to the graveyard. It was weather-boarded with rough oak plank. Andrew Staley had put in a saw mill near the grist mill. The inside of this church was never plastered. The benches were simply slabs with wooden legs and no backs.

The "big meetings" in the church building in the Winter and the camp meetings in the woods in the Summer were depended on to renew religious interest and bring recruits into the church.

One camp meeting worthy of especial notice was held in the woods northwest of town near the large spring back of where Clint Hunter now lives. The camp was a primitive affair and easily set up. As there were no fences or gates no admission was charged. A large burning log pile furnished light, heat, and a common cooking place. The tents were sheets and blankets roughly stretched on poles. The pulpit was a pile of logs. The singing was without instrumental accompaniment, and the prayers loud enough to wake the wilderness solitudes. It was reported that a person standing in the public square of the town on a still night could distinctly hear the words of an old colored woman's prayer at the camp.

The camp grounds were crowded one Sunday morning, people had come for miles around. The people seemed unmoved, the workers were discouraged, the preachers had fired their heaviest artillery. After consultation it was decided that Alexander McCorkle, a local preacher and exhorter should speak to the people. The time had come. McCorkle arose, his arms folded across his breast. He stood until there was a hush of expectation, then with a low and sweet voice he began to sing that soul-stirring rhapsody,

"Sweet rivers of redeeming love,
    Lie just before mine eye,
    Had I the pinions of a dove
I'd to those rivers fly.
    I'd rise superior to my pain
    With joy outstrip the wind,
I'd cross bold Jordan's stormy main,
    And leave the world behind."

Having concluded, he began in a simple way to relate his wonderful experience of conversion. The ice was broken, the hearts of the people began to melt, and all over the camp was the sound of "Hallelujah" and shoutings of "Glory to God"! The psychological moment was on. Seekers of forgiving grace flocked to the mourner's bench and over two hundred professed conversion before the camp meeting ended. This drag net process of course gathered in many things that were not fish, but there were enough genuine accessions to the church so that in 1839 a brick church was built which was considered very fine in its day. It was where Culbertson's Garage now stands. It had a tin-covered belfry, had seats made of dressed lumber with backs, tin reflector lamps on the walls, a wide gallery on three sides so that about 300 people could be seated. There was no organ and no carpet. The Methodists of those days were very strict. No ribbons, no jewelry, no sitting with your girl. The women would be scandalized if a man should be found seated on their side of the house. To remain a member of the church you must pay 25 cents each Quarterly Meeting. You were not in good standing unless you attended family prayers every morning and evening. You might drink and even get drunk. One of the principal distillers was an amen corner member of the church. Morality was not so much emphasized as pious emotion. Old Nelson Lansdale, "Jabess" as he was called, hurried one Sunday morning down to Dr. Obed Horr's to sell his wheat so as not to be late to class meeting. But, mind you, your name was dropped from its roll of membership if you missed class meeting three Sundays in succession without furnishing a lawful excuse. Each attendant at class meeting was given a ticket to the Love Feast at Quarterly Meeting. These were not transferable. To illustrate how strict they were, Samantha Finley presented herself at the door accompanied by her young husband, Frank Finley. She had been faithful, she was admitted by ticket by the door keepers, but her husband was refused admission. Mrs. Finley refused to go in without her husband and also withdrew her membership.

The salary of an itinerant Methodist preacher was two hundred dollars per year for a married man and one hundred for a single man. Out of that he had to furnish his own horse and its keep. But donations were quite common. Some of the more thrifty circuit riders would arrive at home with chickens, eggs, and butter in good supply.

CHAPTER 5.

Primitive Schools.

ON the same outlot on which the church stood, called "The Green", were two school houses. One a little white frame, and the other west of it a small one story brick. The bricks of those days had the clay tramped with oxen and moulded very roughly and the arch brick were burned very hard and out of shape. The old brick schoolhouse had a very large fireplace at the east end. Here George Hartman *kept* school. Spelling, reading, writing, arithmetic and geography were the branches taught. The principal recommendations for a teacher were brute strength and the possession of plenty of good stiff rods. Hartman possessed and used them both. Any man who beats a horse may be arrested. Any one who strikes a child should be fined and imprisoned (Solomon notwithstanding).

Hartman also had tickets for rewards of merit. One merit was given for attendance, five merits for chopping and carrying in an armload of wood, ten for a good lesson, etc. At the end of the year an auction of trinkets and candy was held. One stick of candy sometimes sold for a thousand tickets.

One day a small boy was down behind his desk drawing a picture on the flyleaf of his atlas. Hartman stood in the aisle looking down on him. "Joseph", he said, "give me that atlas. You are fined ten thousand tickets, or will take a whipping." The boy took the whipping rather than part with his coveted tickets.

After cold weather was passed, all of the boys went barefooted. Henry Spain, a tall mischievous lad sat in a seat at the rear. Whenever a bare foot would stray into the aisle, a heavy charge of tobacco spit would strike it with unerring aim. To get even with Henry the small boys mobilized themselves and attacked Henry when school was dismissed. He did not care to hurt any of them, so he took to his heels pursued by a fusillade of poorly aimed stones.

Miss James taught in the white school house. She had a violent temper and was equally savage in the use of the rod. Only the oldest inhabitants remember the old-time school with but one room. With its high slab benches without any backs, the torture of sitting for hours on these seats with no foot rest is not easily forgotten. The little tots sat in front the scholars grading back to the big boys and girls on the rear seats. The course of study consisted of reading, spelling, and figuring as far as the rule of three which consisted in working the rule to find the cube root.

The first grade was called the "A. B. C. Class." They were drilled on learning their letters for months. Then came the "A. B. ab" class. Then they were advanced to the "Baker" grade, and still on they progressed through the monotonous grind to words of eight and ten syllables. Then those who had not become disgusted and quit were allowed to put words together, such as "The ant has legs" "Can the ant run?" All the sentences were droned through without a particle of expression, fixing forever a false habit of reading. The girls with a falsetto straining after effect and the boys with a monotonous style that few recovered from. No one ever thought of teaching the scholars to read first. The old-fashioned manner of spelling was to pronounce each syllable as it was spelled.

Only the rudiments of writing were taught, the finishing touches being given by the traveling writing teacher. The sessions were in the evening. The tuition was usually one dollar per term. The students furnished their own candle, ink, a pen fashioned from the feather of a goose and a blank copy book. The teacher passing from one to the other wrote on the first line such sentences as "Many men of many minds, many birds of many kinds". "Evil communications corrupt good manners": "Comparisons are odious". In the imitations of these copies a universal trait of youthful character was exemplified. The initial line was fairly well done, but each line grew more straggling with numerous blots until the end. Another page would be the same way until the candle had burned down and they all departed for their homes with more ink on their hands than on the paper.

Geography was taught from individual atlases instead of maps and globes as now. The names of states and their capitals were chanted to fix them in memory.

Near dismissal time the teacher was closely watched. When the words were said, "You are dismissed", there was a wild scramble for the door and as the first boy leaped from the door step, he would shout, "First boy out!"

I have thus particularized so that the reader may compare the old with the new manner of "keeping school." I cannot mention all of the old school teachers. You would not know them if I did.

However crude the old methods were, they must be given credit with laying the foundation largely for the present day enlightenment of Mechanicsburg and vicinity. We must not despise the day of small things. The upward progress and attainments of the schools will be noticed further on in this history.

CHAPTER 6.

Cabin Homes.

SOMETHING should now be said about the homes of this pioneer people. Lots in the village were fenced with rails and were very stumpy and filled with roots. The houses as yet were only rude log cabins. The doors were fastened with a latch on the inside. A leather string was fastened to it and passed through a hole in the door. In the homes of the settlers this latch string was always out as an expression of hospitality. The inside furnishings were simple in the extreme. In one end of the kitchen, dining room, sitting room and bedroom combined, was the great wide fireplace. By opening the front and rear doors great logs were drawn in with a horse and rolled onto the fire, where the boiling was done in large iron kettles, roasting and baking in the ashes, and broiling on the clean red coals. At night the fire was buried in the ashes and must never be allowed to go out for if it did they would have to borrow live coals from a neighbor, for matches were not yet invented. Any light that was needed outside of this firelight was produced by laying a piece of cotton in a saucer of grease and lighting it.

As to beds, the well-to-do had bedsteads with turned posts, strung with cords on which were placed straw and feather ticks, covered with homespun blankets, comforts and quilts.

Usually there was a small stand on which was laid the family Bible and hymn book and other books of the scanty library. In the drawer were kept the family keepsakes. The musket with a pouch and powder horn hung over the door. In the corner stood a large spinning wheel and in another, it may be, a loom. These producing a hum of industry had to be their only musical instruments, except in the more ungodly homes there would be a fiddle (not a violin).

The good housewife must be hardy and strong. Besides the care of the children she had to do the cooking, the washing and ironing, mending, carding, heckeling, spinning, weaving, knitting, darning, sewing, patching, rendering lard, making sausage, boiling sap, coloring, etc..

The men must also be sturdy and tireless. It seems now that everything had to be done in the hardest way. The gardens and fields were planted and cultivated with the hoe. The grain cut with a sickle and threshed with a hand flail. Transportation was by wagon, horseback and manback. The forest had to be cleared even though the splendid timber trees were burned just to be rid of them.

It is not strange that these people who had literally to carve their way had little time for literary pursuits. Outside of the Bible and a few very sombre books there was very little to read. A young man presented his fiancee on her birthday with a heavy leather covered volume, entitled "Drelincourt on Death", and it was highly appreciated by her.

Papers and letters were few and far between, for the postage on a letter was 25 cents, which was the price of two chickens or five dozen eggs. Though you could send a letter "collect", this was not in great favor.

If you have never spent a night in one of these cabins you have missed a delightful experience. When the belled cow has been found and driven home, and milked, when the long poles thrown in the street have been chopped and carried in for the fire, when the stock is fed and all the chores are done, when the fire has been replenished and the rag in the saucer lighted, when supper is ready and we gather around the snowy table with highly decorated china ware and wooden-handled knives and forks and great wide spoons, when we eat the mush and milk, a cheerful conversation goes round. No heavy business cares or cares of state to weigh the spirits down. The evening is spent before the blazing fire that up the great wide chimney roars. In the live coals red castles gleam and ships upon the burning waves, and golden glow of sunset skies, or ghost or goblin or angel, as you like. What if the wind is howling around the corner and the dogs lying upon the floor are twitching in their sleep? Does not the tea kettle sing and the cat softly purr by the ingleside? O, who would read at such a time and lose the soul of it. A good and hearty gossip fits it well. Perhaps the blushing maid is twitted of her beau, perhaps a family has lately moved to town. We talk of whence they came and who they are. At last the eyelids will begin to close, the head a little droop. And then! and then! the big high feather bed. O ye gods! Soothed by the gentle warmth and balmy air we fall asleep and nothing know till morn comes on us unawares.

Such were the early experiences in Mechanicsburg homes.

Nothing can teach economy but necessity. Rachel Kelly was the young wife of the tavern keeper, the real estate owner and money man of the town. Miss Amira Wallace was the fiancee of the young store keeper and dude, Jacob R. Ware. Mrs. Kelly and Miss Wallace walked three miles through the woods to a preaching service in a cabin. The point is that they carried their shoes and stockings until they came in sight of the clearing, when they sat down on a log and put them on.

CHAPTER 7.

Broad Humor.

HUMOR is a great conservator of sanity. In every condition a hearty laugh is the very best medicine. The jokes of these early times were broad and formed a part of current history.

Eb Legge was a drunken cobbler. Some of his friends warned him that he would have "snakes", but this had little effect on his drinking. So John Rodebaugh, who worked in the same shop, caught a small garter snake and put it in Eb's tool chest. Eb came staggering in and opened his chest. He sprang back horrified as he saw the snake. At last he had them! "Come here, John, can you see a snake in there?" "Why no, of course not, Eb." Several others had been called in and as had been agreed upon, no one else could see the snake. Eb was convinced, but even this had no effect on his drinking habits.

Uncle Ferril Baker moved his grocery to town in a farm wagon. After unloading his goods, it was dark. To his dismay he found that he had no lock for his door. He propped the door securely on the inside and crawled out through the stick chimney.

Jack Spain, a good fat jovial man was in Uncle Adam Wood's tailor shop having his measure taken for a pair of ample pantaloons. Jack said, "Adam, this was a fine summer for fattening hogs. Acorns are plentiful. We did our butchering last week. Do you folks like spareribs?"

"Yes, Jack, we are very fond of them." "Well, none of our folks will eat them. If you will bring a basket up to our house this evening, you can have ours, and welcome." "All right, Jack, I will surely be there."

This story would lose somewhat of its force were you not told that Adam Woods was a small, sedate, pious, matter-of-fact person. After closing his shop, he climbed the hill with a split hickory basket on his arm, and visions of delicious roast spareribs in his mind. Jack gave him a cordial welcome and filled his basket with rib bones from which all the meat had been eaten. Adam in his astonishment and chagrin almost lost his religion when he exclaimed, "You think you're darned smart."

Jack laughed. Adam did not. When Jack had enjoyed his joke to the full, he took Adam's basket, emptied the bones and filled it with ribs that were not spare of meat.

* * *

John Lupton was a noted borrower. He came over to Sale Horr's house before breakfast, "Sale, I came over to borrow some vinegar." "Well, John, I am sorry to tell you that our vinegar has soured. You can have it as it is, and welcome, John." "Oh, no, Sale, no sour vinegar, no sour vinegar." And he hastened on as Sale stood behind the door laughing.

* * *

Most of the men, even some of the preachers drank intoxicating liquors in those days. A noted, somewhat eccentric divine was holding service in the old log meeting house with its very high pulpit. The congregation had sung a very long hymn and was waiting in breathless expectation for him to arise and begin his discourse, when the preacher, who had fallen asleep, exclaimed, "Fill it up again and charge it to Finley."

* * *

Uncle Claudius Mitchel was carrying a nicely dressed man on his shoulders across a swollen stream and accidentally (?) fell down with him. The gentleman's silk plug went floating down the stream.

* * *

Uncle Claudius was telling in the store that he had just finished digging his potatoes. He said, "They were small, but very few in the hill."

* * *

Argus Cowan was a character. He sold clocks made altogether of wood.. Failing to sell for cash he would trade for a rooster and five dollars to boot. Then when out of sight the rooster was turned loose.

As he went up the street with a basket of eggs one day, a young man in passing him slipped an egg from the basket, and turning threw the egg, hitting Cowan in the back. Cowan whirled and broke on him as he ran every egg he had.

Argus traded horses. After saddles and bridles had been transferred, the man said: "Now, Mr. Cowan, we have traded, tell me what faults this horse has, if any." "Well, I will. He has two bad faults. He is very hard to catch, and he is of no account when he is caught."

Trading horses was very common in those days. When one had traded too much for his own good, it would be said, "He is down to the halter."

*   *   *

Richard Williams was a jolly, fun-loving youth. One blistering hot day in summer he hitched up his sleigh and with sleigh bells jingling astonished the inhabitats by driving up Main street.

At another time choosing a windy day he drove his father's carriage over town with all the curtains loose, scaring the horses.

*   *   *

Colonel Aaron Devers was a monumental liar. Ananias was distanced a mile. He furnished amusement for the whole community. From his cabin on Clover Run he sallied forth to find him a second wife. Finding an old woman who would listen to him he told her that he lived in a mansion with ivory gate posts and a whalebone gate and that he had preserves in the cellar whiter than her nightcap.

When questioned by a man in town as to why he had not delivered some apples bought of him, he said, "See here, Johnnie, I had a thousand bushels piled up in the orchard and a little gnarly bull jumped a ten rail stake and rider fence and eat 'em all up in one night."

Col. Devers said he had a very fine match team of horses, except the black one was a trifle taller than the white one.

Jokers in town would stand him on a box to make political speeches. He would tell with all earnestness of "me and Washington fighting the British side by side. "He called me his 'little yaller plowboy.'"

CHAPTER 8.

Mechanicsburg Incorporated.

MECHANICSBURG was not incorporated until February 27th, 1834. April 5th, following, the first town election was held. Joseph S. Rathbun was elected first Mayor; Isaac Putnam, clerk. The councilmen or trustees elected were Dr. Ebenezer Owen, J. H. Spain, David L. Tullis, Jacob Ware and William Neal. The Council elected John Shepherd, Street Commissioner and Marshal; Dr. Ebenezer

Owen, treasurer; William Kelly, Assessor. They levied a tax of ¼ of 1 per cent for corporation purposes. This yielded an income of $34.82 for 1836.

The total value of the real estate was listed at $6,402. The value of the live stock was $232. Merchant's capital and notes $9,830. Joseph C. Brand had $3,000, Jesse S. Bates $1,000, Obed Horr $4,000, Ware and McCorkle $1,800. These were the capitalists of those days. In 1880, only 44 years later, the total valuation had grown to about $800,000. In 1917 it had increased to about $1,500,000. The ratio of increase being an average of about $20,000 per year. There has been a slow but steady growth, no boom, but the town has grown as does the enduring oak.

During 1839 and 40 the salary of D. F. Spain as treasurer was $1.50 per year.

William Kelly the tavern keeper and Constable was a very large man and this coupled with his office made him a terror to children. Mothers frightened their children into obedience by threatening to "tell Kelly." He was described as being able to "stand lots of rest". So that the phrase for idleness was, "I am helping Kelly." While he was landlord of the tavern there were wild "goings on." A large oak tree stood in the square in front of the tavern. Such characters as Pete Shaul from Sodom, Colonel Devers, Dan Hash and Alex Henry from Clover Run would come in on election days and would set a jug of whisky at the foot of the tree and then all would go about a mile away, to a point near the Brittin farm east of town. "One, two, three" was counted, when the wild scramble started. The man who got to the jug first had it, provided he could silence all objections with his fist. Accusations of unfair play easily started and if not from this from some other cause a fight was begun between the factions and many knock downs, black eyes and bloody noses resulted.

Gaming seems to be natural to all conditions and places. Mechanicsburg was no exception. Usually the whole night was spent in gambling. . Kelly was very successful until the liquor began to get in its work, when he invariably lost all he had gained. No election passed without drunkenness and fighting.

CHAPTER 9.

The Big Fight.

IT is perfectly natural that men should covet and admire that which they most need in their physical existence. For this reason the pioneer who has to labor and endure prizes physical ability most of all. His life is nearer the plane of the wild beast. In these primitive times the man who could show his superiority by over-coming his antagonist was the hero of the community. This demonstration of manhood as it was called must of course be made without weapons other than what nature had endowed him with. These conditions obtained in all early settlements. Men have been known to ride on horseback for thirty miles to pull off a fight.

So far as known the fiercest and hardest fought battle of this kind in Mechanicsburg took place in the public square on November 8th, 1837, between Solomon Weaver and Philip Groves. They were both large and powerfully built. Weaver lived on the Darby Plains, that stretch away to the southeast, Groves on Clover Run, a region of white clay hills to the southwest. Weaver was the father of a large family of children. Anna, the oldest born was a comely maiden of eighteen summers, healthy and robust. At the neighborhood huskings and dances dressed in her homespun gown she was admired by many suitors, but it was evident that her heart was with James Groves. He came on horseback twelve miles to pay his visits which lasted from Saturday evening to Monday morning. Being a son of Phil Groves who resided in the disreputable neighborhood of Clover Run made his frequent visits somewhat distasteful to her father.

On this particular morning, not being in the most amiable mood, he had saddled his horse and mounting rode close up in front of the cabin door and called in a loud voice for "Ann," who came to the door.

"What do you want, father?"

"See here, I'm tired of that young clover blossom comin' here so often."

"Father?"

"I mean what I say."

"He's a nice young man."

"Nice enough I reckon, but look where he would take you to live."

"Father, you talk like we were married."

"Well, what does he come here so much for?" She was about to shut the door.

"Listen to me! I'm going to town and I'm goin' to whip Jim Groves' daddy. I wouldn't fight a little stripplin' like Jim."

"Please don't father. Please don't and I will stay here with you as long as you want me." She reached up and caught the bridle rein.

"Now, now! don't be silly, little girl, I was just jokin'. I am going to town to vote."

"Father, if I let you go, you won't get drunk, will you?"

"Of course I won't Now let go. My! but you're purty. I don't wonder the boys want to get you away from me. Let go, little one."

"Hold up your hand and promise me you won't drink a drop and won't fight Mister Groves."

"Well, Ann, I guess I will have to promise all that. I don't want to ride over you."

"Now remember."

And as he rode away, turning he saw her over his shoulder, standing watching as if she were a good angel. Had he been a philosopher he would have realized that gentle, tender love was stronger than strength, can melt the hardest heart and break the strongest will.

He rode with loose rein, absorbed in thought, barely giving his riding enough attention to keep his horse headed toward the west. The man and the beast were contending within him. Temptation comes from the lower or animal nature. It is the province of the divine soul to subdue and control. The good angel by the help of love for his daughter had won in the great man heart. Solomon Weaver firmly resolved that he would religiously keep his promise to Anna. The sombre silence of the almost unbroken forest except here and there a settler's cabin allowed him communion with his better self. Undisturbed communion with nature always has a quieting effect. So that when he arrived at the Darby creek ford near the mill all enmity had died within him. The pitifulness of these inward struggles is that they must be renewed, even as long as we live in these earthly bodies. We are never safe from the assaults of temptation and evil. A favorable circumstance that gave him further time for meditation was that his horse drank longer of the clear, pure water of the brook.

By this time the manhood in him was in control. He followed the dog fennel track up through what was given the name of Main street. He would do a little trading at the store, vote, and go back home. Unfortunately he dismounted and hitched his horse to a small tree in front of a little log shop on the top of which was a board, on which was scrawled the legend, "Bill Albason, Boot and Shoe Shop." The day being fine the door was open. Albason came out with his leather apron on, and extended his stained hand, "Sol, howde? Fine day? How are all the folks? Come in, your boots are done." "Bill, I didn't expect they were done. I haven't the money now to pay for them." "Never mind that, come in and try them on, your credit's good." "Well, I will try them on." They entered together. After they were inside, Albason approached Weaver in a confidential manner. "Say, Sol, I suppose you heard I was running for constable. Here is a ticket. I would like to have you vote for me. Say, Sol, for all its such a fine day, it's a little chilly riding. Here's a little whisky, it will warm you up a bit."

"No, Bill, excuse me this time. I promised Ann that I wouldn't. Sol Weaver keeps his word." Albason put on a look of mock surprise, "Sol Weaver! Well! well! when did you get tangled up in your women's apron strings?"

Notwithstanding the refusal he uncorked the bottle, saying, "It's good. I got it this very morning from the distillery across the creek."

Weaver would have resented this impertinence had not the smell of the red liquor reached him. As it was he allowed himself to parley with the temptation. "Bill, I think I better not." Albason poured some in a glass and held it out toward Weaver.

"Well, for friendship's sake, I will drink just a swallow." The man in him lost this time.

"Pour me out another, Bill."

"That's right, you are your own man. That's what you

are, Sol. Say, Old Phil Groves is in town. I · heard him bragging that he was going to beat your life out. He said you mistreated his son, Jim, when he was there to see your gal."

"Did you hear him say that, did you say?"

"Yes, I did."

The blood began to surge through Solomon Weaver's heart and flame in his cheek. The animal nature in him was thoroughly aroused and beat down all opposition. He strode through the door and up the street toward the tavern where the election was held. By a strange mischance Phil Groves was standing on the step. Weaver approaching bluntly said, "I heard you said you would beat me up."

"I can do it, Sol Weaver. My boy Jim is just as good as your gal, any day."

"If you think you can whip me you have a good chance to try it right now."

Kelly, the tavern keeper and constable hearing the quarrel stepped out.

"See here, boys, no fighting near the polls. Come out in the square if you want to fight. Follow me."

Kelly, who was a very large and powerful man and a perfect daredevil himself, marked off a circle in the dirt and leaves, then drew a line through the center of it with his heavy cane which he carried for a mace.

"Now, boys, everything we ask is that there be fair play. You must have no weapons. I will search you."

All clubs and stones were removed from the ring. The rumor spread like wildfire. Men and boys with here and there a woman came running from all directions shouting, "Fight! A fight!" And soon the square was surrounded with a pushing and jostling crowd all eager to get where they could see. Kelly raised his cane. Listen to me! If either one of you hollers 'enough', the other one must stop, not another lick. Remember now, or you will wish you had. Take off your coats."

They took them off and laid them on two stumps.

"Now, toe the line. When I count three, begin. *One, two, three."*

Weaver aimed a vicious blow at Groves' face, who quickly ducked and before Weaver could recover his balance, laid a heavy blow on Weaver's breast. That sent him backward for

several steps, but rushing, they clinched. Weaver having a slight
advantage in weight forced Groves back to the ring of onlookers
who began to scatter, Kelly shouting for them to get farther
back. The combatants fell to the ground, clawing, scratching
and biting. Groves releasing himself sprang to his feet and
began kicking Weaver, trying to stamp him in the face. Weaver
shielding himself with his arm, managed to get on his feet also.
Here they began pounding each other with their hard clenched
fists without regard to strategy. Blood flowed freely from
Groves' nose and mouth at which there was a wild cheer from
the Darby plains crowd.

Groves maddened by pain and angered by the shouts, with
a fierce blow knocked Weaver down. Here a wild shout broke
from the Clover Run sympathizers. Before Weaver could rise
Groves was on him. His right hand being disabled by the blow
that felled Weaver he began pounding him with his left. Kelly
seeing the disadvantage of Weaver, commanded them to rise
and take their breath. At a signal to renew the combat they
went at it with renewed fierceness. Kelly was censured for his
interference but was too formidable for any one to let him hear
their censure. The battle went on for an hour or more. It is
not necessary to repeat the sickening details. It was evident that
one or the other would be killed. Groves backing away a few
steps ran up to Weaver giving him a vicious kick in the breast
breaking three ribs. Weaver fell and Groves was again upon
him. It seemed but a question of a few moments when Weaver
would be killed, but by a quick motion he grabbed Groves' eyes
with both hands. Groves, completely blinded, fell over on his
side, and the cry went up that they were both killed. The doctors were hastily sent for, Doctors Horr, Cheney and Lawler.
Horr came first. He looked at the battered men lying on the
ground. Blood ran from Weaver's mouth, Groves' eyes were
lying on his cheeks. Dr. Horr, thinking them both dead, was
horrified, and exclaimed, "Kelly, why did you allow this?" Not
waiting for a reply he examined the men and found them both
breathing faintly. Feeling that the reader is already horrified
by the ghastly details, I will only say that by careful nursing and
blest with strong constitutions they both, recovered.

The details have thus been dwelt upon that an idea may be
had of these fierce encounters, showing a phase of the times.

No election ever passed without a number of fights and much drunkenness. And, strangely, Christmas, the anniversary of the Prince of Peace was made a day of drunken revelry and fighting.

The great fight did not end the love story. Solomon Weaver instead of holding enmity against Philip Groves expressed his admiration of him. So Anna sent a little agitated note to James that if he still wished to come to see her he would be welcome.

CHAPTER 10.

Old Documents.

MR. O. C. Hupp has kindly placed in our hands a very old book. It is dated 1837 and is the record of the Goshen Township Clerk. Many of its musty pages are taken up with wordy indentures of children. This child slavery is happily now unknown and will therefore need some explanation. This relic of the dark ages of the past was in the early history of Mechanicsburg commonly practiced. Some of its old and well remembered citizens were victims of this inhuman practice. The original intention was to bind out young men to learn a particular trade, but through an unholy greed boys and girls from six to fifteen years of age were bound in the most abject servitude to work on the master's farm and in their mistress' kitchen, very often enduring oppressive and cruel treatment, until they were of age. For all this labor, at the end of their servitude they were given a cheap Bible and a suit of clothes. Among the stipulations of the indenture, drawn up with great legal formality, the poor child was to receive each year six weeks of schooling. As it stated they were to be taught to read and write and figure as far as the single rule of three, as it was expressed. Many of the old Medieval terms were still in use. They were known as master and servant. They were to be instructed in the "art, trade, mystery or occupation" of some particular craft. Sometimes the "mystery" was how to feed a hog, or wash dishes, we suppose. The world moves. This slavery of our children has become a half forgotten reminiscence. Among the poor children who were thus bound out we find a family by the name of "Grubb." But on turning to another page of the book it was seen that this family was warned by the authorities to leave town for fear they would become a charge upon it. Again the world moves. Such a proceeding now would be considered inhuman.

Mr. George Darling has loaned us a copy of the first newspaper published in the place, Vol. 1, No. 13. Dated December 15th, 1870. E. Mettles, editor and publisher. Office Riddle Building, Main street. Terms, cash in advance, $1.25 per year. Advertising one week $7.00 per column. No patent sides. The corporation officers mentioned therein were, Mayor, J. D. Rodebaugh; Clerk, T. E. Shepherd; Marshal, J. Ernest; County Clerk, V. Horr; Councilmen, J. S. Magruder, Thos. Morgan, Chas Baxter, J. C. Sceva, and Sanford Darling.

Under the heading of "Deaths", we read, "Died on the 14th of December, 1870, Nathaniel Sceva, aged 63." In those times he was considered an old man. His memory is honored by what he accomplished in those years and by his esteemed family.

In the editorial we find, "As the Atlantic cable has become so notorious for lying, when we find there is any truth in a cable despatch we will publish it as a curiosity."

A notice reads, "There are yet a large number of our country friends who have not paid up. We will take wood, butter, eggs, or any kind of produce. Come along, who will be the first to pay?"

The most striking thing we notice is that the advertisers are all dead or have quit the business.

Notice these,

James Fullington, President of the Union Fair Association; Thomas Davis, Secretary; Thomas Buffington, Grocer; J. N. Shaul, wagon maker; C. A. Baker & Bros., Tailors; W. B. Wilkinson, Dry Goods merchant; D. W. C. Holland, Drayman; Thos. Morgan & Co., Hardware; Williams & Davis, of the Farmer's Bank; J. L. Nation, Drayman; Martin & Hunter, Grocers; Daniel Ernest, Silversmith; C. H. Newcomb, Undertaker; Robert J. Lowe, Barber; Wm. Williams, Insurance; Culbertson & Murray, Livery & Feed Stable and Buggy Makers; Williams & Sceva, Dry Goods merchants; Legge & Rodebaugh, Boots & Shoes; J. L. Magruder & Son, Harness Makers; Taylor & Walters, druggists; P. W. Alden, Dry Goods, These changes have come so gradually that they are hardly noticed but in looking back forty-seven years it is most striking.

These old newspapers show very forcibly the mutations that are continually being wrought by time. It produces a longing in the mind of the writer to fix and perpetuate the history of every one of those who have been prominently connected with the progress of our town, but such cannot be done in the bounds of a volume such as this, and we would not attempt to particularly notice one unless we could be impartial and mention all.

CHAPTER 11.

Main Street in 1840.

GET a mental picture of Main street in 1840. It had not as yet been blessed with any of its great fires. Look first at that very long, one-story, creepy frame with the end to the street. It is on the west side of Main street something over two hundred feet above the square. Nick Wynant has his cabinet shop with the big black bear in there. Just south of it is Dr. Lawler's orchard. Below that is the two-story brick, Lawler's Tavern. Farther down that long one-story building running to Sandusky street is "Long Ornery." Look across Sandusky and you see "AMERICAN HOUSE" painted on the whole length of the frame building. It is Joiner's Tavern. There is a bar in the front room and a small grocery in the lower corner. That frame building with a ledge in front on which loafers sat, is T. J. Glendenning's tailor shop. Step out and look above in the upper window. Do you see a tall, bent form with long gray hair? That is Eli Alden. He is slowly turning a large wooden wheel. He is trying to invent perpetual motion, a motion that will go on without stop or diminution forever just from the initial impulse like the motions of the earth. He says that he has discovered it, but it will stop.

The frame building on the alley is Ware's and McCorkle's store. Across the alley is another little frame and then that white building with the eaves to the street is Azro Mann's residence. Although he was a man of good principle, he said he believed that there was a hell and that he was going to it. Believers in predestination usually think it is in their favor.

Now we come to the most primitive drug store you ever knew, high and narrow wooden steps in front, lighted with a single tallow dip at night. If you should wish to buy anything Uncle Bobbie would carry the light and find it for you. It is Robert Jones' drug store.

That little unpainted building farther down is Albason's Shoe Shop. That is his pile of firewood in the street.

Cross over the street. That building is Jones' Hall. Williams Brothers have their dry goods store in the first story. The hall above is reached by rickety outside stairs. This is used for all secular assembly purposes, either by day or early candle light.

On up the street are Jim Carlton's tailor shop and Dad Magruder's harness shop. Look long at that log building across the Magruder alley for that is Spain's Tavern. Back in the alley is the Post Office. The frame building on the southeast corner of the public square is Levi Rathbun's store. There is a very small assembly room over it with the entrance on Sandusky street. On the northeast corner of the square the lot is vacant. Next above is Owen & Keyes drug store (still standing as Venrick's tin shop). Then Dr. Ebenezer Owen's dwelling.

To complete the picture we have the militia coming down the street. That rather tall, slender, sandy-complexioned man is Colonel Bates. He steps or rather bounces backward facing his troops. On his hip hangs his sword. He is girdled with a long red sash. He is a soldier only in name, yet no military hero was ever prouder than he. Nothing was ever accomplished by his army except the scaring of the horses on the streets.

This is a picture of Mechanicsburg as she was.

In the above-mentioned year, 1840, a society of Baptists was organized, and in 1846 they erected a one-story frame meeting house twenty feet wide and thirty feet long. The lot on which it was built fronted on Locust street, or alley it was then. It had a peculiar style of church architecture. The high pulpit was placed in the front, between the two entrance doors, so that when one came late the pulpit must be passed, and the audience faced. The floor being uncarpeted, the confusion was complete. Old Uncle Jimmie Woodward stood in the doorway to ring the bell, which he did with great punctuality. The church was all in all to him and Aunt Dollie, his wife. Perhaps the planks of the seats were no harder than boards usually are, but it always seemed as if they were, and the mourners' benches more tire-some to the kneeler. These Baptists were a good substantial people, but none of them had a vision and in a few years the society became extinct.

*   *   *

In 1849 occurred the great rush to the California gold fields. Those going from this vicinity as far as can be remembered were Milton Cheney, William Patrick, Dr. James Williams, Benjamin Taylor, John Legge and William Black. The journey, was made across the plains and the great American desert in schooners (covered wagons). Some of them came back better off than when they started. One William Black never did come back. One evening as these men were sitting before their camp fire, Black made the remark that he intended to shoot the first squaw that came along. His companions thought nothing of it, thinking that he was joking. But the foolhardy man actually shot a squaw who was passing. The outraged and enraged Indians surrounded the camp and by an interpreter demanded that the one committing the murder should be given up to them, or they would kill the whole party. This they were compelled reluctantly to do. The Indians took Black, bound him and actually skinned him alive.

CHAPTER 12.

The Underground Railroad.

AS a great moral upheaval the anti-slavery movement in Mechanicsburg, began in 1833 in this wise:

Jacob R. Ware and Alexander McCorkle took a drove of horses and sold them throughout the South. At Vicksburg, while waiting for a boat, they visited a slave auction where a young slave woman was being sold. Afterward her little boy was offered for sale. The young mother got down on her knees to her purchaser and begged him to buy her boy that they might not be separated. The hard-hearted man struck her and pushed her away, saying he would buy what he pleased.

Mr. Ware said to himself, "Not if I can help." At home he became what was at that time called "a black abolitionist," circulating literature, employing speakers, and making his home a station on the underground railroad. Many hundred colored people passed on this line to a refuge in Canada.

Mr. Ware, fearing imprisonment and loss of property through the operation of the infamous fugitive slave law which made a slave catcher of every citizen of the free states, employed Udnah H. Hyde as a brave and skillful conductor to pilot the fugitives to the next station. Mr. Hyde was able to make the proud boast that he never lost one of the 513 whom he assisted.

The roll of the early members of the Abolition party here included the names of W. P. Alden, Levi Rathbun, Azro Mann, David Rutan, Robert Wilson, John M. Davis, Charles Taylor, Obed Horr, Orin Mann, and others.

At great risk and cost to themselves these and later anti-slavery people acted the Good Samaritan to these colored fugitives who told many pitiful stories of the hardships and abuse endured while in bondage. At one time twenty-four men came through in one gang. Often a single woman would be fleeing for liberty alone.

The underground railroad continued to operate until President Lincoln's proclamation freed the slaves.

In 1857 occurred the Addison White episode. The infamous Fugitive Slave law passed at the dictation of the slave holding states made the penalty for refusing to aid in the capture and return of a fugitive slave either fine or imprisonment or both. The slave holding oligarchy also dictated to the Supreme Court the fearful Dred Scott decision, so that it was doubly dangerous to defend or assist the slave fleeing for his liberty.

The celebrated Addison White rescue case was a forceful illustration of the intolerable conditions which soon resulted in the terrible civil war in 1860-65.

A very large and strong and therefore valuable negro slave, Addison White, arrived in Mechanicsburg in 1857. Instead of taking him on, Udnah Hyde hired him to work for him. Addison was anxious to have his wife escape and come to him. Charles Taylor imprudently wrote a letter to her, informing her of her husband's whereabouts. This letter of course fell into the master's hands. Several days after this Addison was in the front room of the Hyde house pulling on his boots when a squad of three U. S. marshals and seven deputies passed the window. He quickly sprang to the ladder and ascended to the loft of the cabin.

To prevent escape the deputies were stationed on all sides of the house. The three marshals without stopping to knock pushed open the door and entered. One of them by the name of Eliott noticed a board of the loft floor move. He raised his gun and fired a load of buckshot through it and springing to the ladder imprudently ascended. As his head appeared above the opening Addison fired, the rifle ball struck the barrel of Eliott's gun and was slightly deflected, so that only his ear was severely wounded. He fell to the floor below, exclaiming, "I am a dead man." Hyde, a very excitable man, fumed and swore, "Why didn't you go on up and get him? Damn you!" "Manda, tell Reuben to come here." He whispered in his son's ear — he started out the door, but was stopped and sent back. Hyde whispered to his daughter, Manda. Then in a loud voice said, "Feed the Chickens, Manda, they haven't been fed this morning." The ruse worked, when she had a good start she began to run. One of the marshal's shouted after her, "You, girl, stop, or I will shoot." Her black eyes snapped as she shouted back, "Shoot and be durned!" And away she fled and the people in the "abolition hole," Mechanicsburg, were notified of the situation.

Many of the citizens came out to the rescue. The marshals instead of trying further to capture the negro, contented themselves with arresting those who seemed most forward in aiding him. Charles Taylor, Edward Taylor, Russell Hyde and Hiram Gutridge were taken in a carriage. William Pangborn, a lawyer of our town, came up to the carriage and said to the prisoners, "You dont have to go, just say the word." One of the officers said, with an oath, "That's talk."

The marshals started immediately as if going to Urbana, but on the top of Clark's hill turned south. The country from end to end was now thoroughly aroused like it was with John Brown's raid. David Rutan and Oliver Colwell on horseback overtook them. The carriages were stopped and these two men were driven back by threats and pointed revolvers. The marshals also threatened that if they were molested they would kill the prisoners who were manacled together two and two. Rescue parties were sent out from many points. The rumor was that they were to be taken to Kentucky and mobbed. The excitement grew with the suspense. It was a high-handed and unheard of proceeding, the abduction without legal process of free American citizens. Party lines were obliterated, indignation flamed. The people in the North were in no temper for such an outrage. The two brothers, Charles and Edward Taylor secretly agreed that if they attempted to cross the Ohio river with them, they would each seize an officer and jump overboard into the river.

The posse with the prisoners were tracked through Catawba Station, Summerford and South Charleston, where they assaulted the sheriff of Clark County. From here they passed through Cedarville to a point east of Xenia. Their intention was plainly revealed by their course, to cross the Ohio river into Kentucky. The Greene County sheriff and posse intercepted them here and took the U. S. marshals and locked them up in the jail at Springfield. The prisoners were brought back to Mechanicsburg. The case was afterward settled by the citizens buying Addison for $800. Our late Thomas E. Shepherd, a member of the Bates Silver Cornet Band (Known as the 66th Ohio) was one day talking with a wounded Confederate soldier from Kentucky whom he had helped to bring in from the field The wounded man asked Shepherd where he was from. The reply was, "Mechanicsburg, Ohio." "Did you ever hear of the Addison White case?" "I surely did." "I want to ask you whether you know the little girl that I threatened to shoot as she ran to give the alarm. She surely had nerve." "I guess I know her pretty well, she is my wife."

CHAPTER 13.

An Era of Improvement.

WE have now passed the pioneer stage of our little city. From this time on began its substantial growth and improvement.

One of the great factors of its development was the construction of the Springfield, Mt. Vernon and Pittsburgh Railroad. It was opened to traffic between Springfield and Delaware in the year 1850. On account of the meagerness of its

resources its initials were facetiously interpreted to be, "Small
Means and Poor Pay." The $30,000 which Goshen Township
contributed to its construction was considered a great sum at
the time, but it has proved to be a wonderfully good investment.

It is not necessary to mention other abortive attempts to in-
crease the railroad facilities. The range of hills West of us
has prevented any success in that line. Yankee Hill between
here and Urbana attains a height of 386 feet above the level
of Darby, or 1,489 feet above sea level. So the community has
to be content with one Railroad running Northeast and Southwest. The first station agent came here from Delaware. Captain Vincent Hunter succeeded him. Under his administration,
the depot was moved from Main street to the lot farther East,
so the trains would have room to stop without obstructing the
crossing.

Mechanicsburg was greatly helped by several great fires
which wiped out many of the ancient and disreputable buildings,
making room for new and better structures. Such were the burning of the old American House and the Blackburn bakery which
cleaned up many shacks on the West side. Then the Jones'
Hall fire. I will digress to say that there are a number of other
buildings that would burn good.

A very disastrous conflagration was the burning of the
Drill Factory building on South Main Street.

In the early days the fire company was a volunteer organization which included every man and woman in town. Instead
of an engine every one carried a bucket of water to be thrown
on the fire. Nearly every person was a fire chief at this time,
all shouting at once what should be done. It may have been
hard on the people's cisterns and wells and buckets but it was
often effective. One would pump until out of breath, the
others standing in a line to pass the buckets of water, this line
extending to the man on the top of the ladder. The empty
buckets were not passed back but thrown to the ground, more
often than not striking some excited fireman on the head.

This is in striking contrast to our present day, well organ-
·ized fire company composed of 12 brave lads who earn much more
than their meagre $1.50 each per call. The company at present
is, Chief, H. H. Darling; Assistant Chief, Dr. E. R. Stockwell;
Engineer, George Darling; Assistant Engineer, Ed. Morris;·

Driver, Joe Anderson; Ed. Conway, Ralph Francis, Charles Palmer, Harry Dickey, Charles Hanley, Joe Thompson, Martin Moore.

In 1875 The Mechanicsburg Machine Company was incorporated. In 1876 was begun the manufacture of the Baker Grain Drill. Three years later the capital was increased to $125,000 and a large three story brick building and foundry were erected. This was a fatal move as the management had not the experience and business ability to manage a concern of this magnitude. A large output of the drills before they were fully perfected was a mistake that could not be retrieved. The complete bankruptcy of the concern and the enormous and iniquitous cost of liquidation left a double liability on the stockholders. This gave Mechanicsburg a blow from which recovery was slow. A distrust of stock concerns made public enterprise difficult. Had the substantial building on South Main street remained the disaster would in time have been overcome, but unfortunately it was sold to a non-resident at a ruinous price and afterwards burned to the ground, not without suspicion as to the origin of the fire.

In September 1869 the first Central Ohio Fair was held on the Fair Grounds in the West end of town. These grounds are unsurpassed in natural beauty and adaptability. The fifty acres consisted of an elevated grove of natural forest trees, the shady sloping hills forming a grassy amphitheater overlooking the half mile race track. A very large spring of clear, mineral water bubbling up in a large circular terraced marble basin and piped to all parts of the park, furnished an ample supply of water. A picturesque view through the trees toward the east disclosed a silver, willow-rimmed lake. The fame of this Fair spread far and wide, bringing our town into prominence. People attended from all parts of the state, the patronage often rivalling that of the State Fair.

CHAPTER 14.

The Civil War.

SUCH incidents as the Addison White case described heretofore aided in bringing on the great civil war between North and South. The shots fired at Fort Sumter broke the shackles from every slave. Patriotism was aroused. The response was quick to Lincoln's call for 75,000 men for 90 days. John Horr, Edward Taylor, Thomas Owen, Carp Groves, Peter Hardman and Melvin Kenfield were the first to enlist.

This community has the proud record that no draft was ever required. Those were terrible days. The post office was thronged at every mail by friends anxiously waiting for some word from the front. Hope and fear struggled in the hearts of all. How the soldiers suffered with homesickness and exposure can never be known. Statistics show that more of them died from these causes than were killed in battle. In the call to arms many families were left with an inadequate support. These were cared for by our patriotic citizens. The following is a list of those who died in the service: Dwight Horr, H. M. Snodgrass, Stephen Baxter, Clifton Sewell, Wilson, Henry and Francis Brittin, Edward Taylor, Joseph Canady, Samuel Brinnon, John Kohler, Lawler Chidister, James Boulton, Joseph Newcomb, Azro Mann, Robert Osborn, Ezra Allen, Alex Henry, Harrison Waldron, Channing Horr, Orlando Lawler, John Lane, Joseph Shepherd, Ruben Alden, William Tullis, Mason Tucker, Peter Miller, John Cawood, Samuel Jones, Ira and George Sargeant, Thomas Hudson, Melville Kenfield, Zane Stephenson, George Huffman, William Miller, Taylor Darrow, Samuel Johnston, Isaac Groves. Died of disease, 20. Killed, 19. Total, 39.

The members of the Grand Army of the Republic and Women's Relief Corps still remind us of the terrific struggle which united the nation and freed the slaves. The whole community on May 30th each year unites with these patriotic orders to strew flowers on the graves of our soldier dead. Did space permit we would gladly mention all who enlisted in their country's service.

CHAPTER 15.
Modern Mechanicsburg.

THE corporation is now one mile square, containing 640 acres, lying on three hills. These give it an excellent and healthful drainage and a beauty unsurpassed. Urbana, the county seat, is ten miles west. Springfield is 18 miles to the southwest, Columbus is 32 miles east and Delaware 33 miles northeast. It is surrounded by the beautiful township of Goshen, named after the garden spot of Egypt of that name. If this were appropriate in its primitive state, how much more so now with its fertile fields, elegant homes and immense teeming barns. The present population with its nearby suburbs is about two thousand. Its well kept houses, velvety lawns, its streets overarched with noble maple trees, make it a beautiful and desirable residence town. Add to this the more than average intelligence of the citizens and you have an almost ideal place in which to live. The sidewalks and gutters are of concrete. Main street has brick paving (the first in the county).

The churches and schools hold the center of interest, as they should. Unlike many towns Mechanicsburg is not over-churched. There are but four white Protestant churches, the Methodist Episcopal, Methodist Protestant, Episcopalian and Christian Science. There is one Catholic Church and two colored churches, the Methodist and Baptist.

CHURCHES.

The early history of the Methodist church is given in sufficient detail in a former chapter, No. 4. It remains to say that in 1858 they dedicated a brick church on East Sandusky. This had a Sunday School room and a number of class rooms on the first floor and a good sized auditorium on the second floor. It served its purpose well for 36 years and was then sold to the colored Baptists.

In 1894 the present beautiful and commodious house of worship was dedicated. The Sunday School room with a large balcony and adjoining class rooms can be thrown together with the auditorium and can accommodate a large congregation. They have a strong organization with a large and loyal membership.

The Methodist Protestants were organized in 1853 with an enrollment of 92. Of this number Joseph Ware is the only charter member now living, who is still a member. Just prior to this date the M. E. Church of this place was torn with anti-slavery agitation and much of the bitterness still remained. Rev. S. P. Keserta, a young M. P. minister thought he saw a fine opening for a church of that denomination and so reported to the Ohio Annual Conference, which sent him here the following February and he held a successful revival which resulted in the organization of a church with an enrollment of 92 members. Most of them were the children of anti-slavery families, who were among the best people of the place.

The trustees elected at that time were Professor W. D. Henkle, J. R. Ware, F. A. Kinley and William Purtlebaugh. The stewards were David Rodebaugh, Alexander McConkey and George Wolf.

This church was never a mission in the sense of receiving outside aid. It did not make the mistake so often made in buying a cheap lot in an impossible location, but did make a similar one by allowing a Masonic Hall to be placed over the building erected on the corner of Sandusky and Walnut streets. This, the first church building, was dedicated in 1855. In 1873 this was decorated and improved at an expense of $1,800. In 1890 the Masonic Hall was purchased and the old building completely torn down and on the site the present beautiful and modern house of worship was erected. In 1873 Rachael Kelly endowed the Sunday School in the sum of $1,637.

We mention a unique feature of this church that may be useful to other churches. A large and beautiful white marble tablet is placed on the wall of the auditorium inscribed with the names of persons who wish to perpetuate their membership by leaving bequests, the interest of which shall pay their church dues for all time. It is a monument to their memory much more beneficial and perpetual than a shaft in the cemetery. Their names are also continued on the register as active members.

Joseph Ware has perhaps served the longest term as Sunday School superintendent of any one in the United States, having served 56 years without a break. Charles L. McCorkle has been one of the superintendents for 35 years.

The Protestant Episcopal Society dedicated their church building on South Main Street in 1894. It is designated "The Church of Our Savior." Both the exterior and interior are very attractive. During the twenty-three years of its existence it has lost very heavily by death and removal. Its membership is very active 'and loyal. This the youngest of the churches has been welcomed into the brotherhood of the religious organizations.

The Christian Scientists, although they have no church building as yet, hold regular meetings each Sabbath in a hall over the Hanley & Maddex store. Their congregation is made up of excellent people.

The St. Michael's Catholic church on Walnut street is a brick edifice dedicated in 1888. It has a large membership which is extremely faithful in attendance on its services. They have a great many members in the country surrounding the town. Although we do not have access to any records, we think this church began holding services here in 1859.

The African Methodist Episcopal Church is on the corner of Walnut and Race streets and has a faithful membership.

The colored Baptist society occupies the old brick M. E. building on East Sandusky street. It is nicely decorated on the interior and is fitted with electric lights.

SCHOOLS.

The children of the early settlers secured what education they could in private or tuition schools, the pedagogue receiving the tuition as his compensation. Only the common branches were taught. "Bobbie" Wilson, a kind and affable Irishman built a school house back of the "green" on Race street. He was "keeping school" here when in 1847 what was then called the Akron law, now perfected in the Union Schools Laws of Ohio, was passed. Uncle Bobbie and W. D. Henkle were made superintendents at this time. Having no school building sufficient for the various grades, they met in rented rooms about town. Strange to say this advance in education met with strong opposition from those who objected to paying "poor children's tuition."

In 1865 two acres of land were purchased of Nelson Lansdale on High street, and the first "union" school building was erected. In 1871 an addition was built. In 1894 this building was torn down and the present handsome and commodious building took its place, at a cost in money and material of approximately thirty thousand dollars. This fine building with tastily kept grounds is an education in refinement and good taste to the pupils. However, this large building has become inadequate for the accommodation of the enlarged school since the township centralization. Had not the European war so stimulated prices of material, an additional building costing probably sixty thousand·dollars would have been built. However this may cause delay, it cannot prevent this obvious necessity. There are seventeen teachers and 540 pupils.

F. S. Fuson has been properly styled the father of our present graded system. He first arranged for graduation exercises and the presentation of diplomas in 1881. He also gave a stimulus to normal work by giving those who graduated here a chance to teach at home and lending assistance in finding places for them in other schools.

We wish to most heartily commend the present superintendent, Professor Bert Highlands for his many additions and reforms in educational methods, especially in the practical application of education to everyday living, not only in manual training, but in morality and temperance. Eighty-five per cent of the boys who used tobacco have been induced to quit. Profanity is almost entirely suppressed. The evil effects of alcoholic stimulants are shown in an earnest and effective way. Industry and helpfulness are encouraged.

·ATTRACTIONS.

A feature of the town of especial interest is Matinee Park, formerly known as The Central Ohio Fair Grounds. It is proposed to erect a permanent assembly hall here. It still has the abundant spring of mineral water, a splendid half mile racing track and beautiful oak shade trees. The annual Chautauqua assembly is held here each August and all outdoor celebrations and picnics. It is owned by a stock company of citizens of which Harry S. Bailey is president.

On the South shore of beautiful Shadow Lake lies Lakeside Park. The lake covers some ten acres and is sixty feet deep, furnishing recreation, boating, fishing and bathing. Many from a distance visit these grounds in the Summer season.

To the southwest rise several steep hills to an altitude of 160 feet. On them is situated Maple Grove Cemetery, purchased and laid out in 1870. The first grave was a double one in which were interred William and Elizabeth Tway, man and wife. The hills are now covered with the white monuments of the dead. On the highest summit stands the marble figure, heroic size, of a private soldier looking intently toward the battlefields of the South. This monument, dedicated to the soldiers and sailors of the Civil War, was conceived and planned by Mrs. Mary Rutan Moore and with the co-operation of many patriotic citizens was carried to completion. Mrs. Moore, though overtaken by sickness, did not relax her efforts, but by a wonderful will power continued her interest until, assisted by appreciative friends to the unveiling, her feeble hand pulled the cord and unveiled the wonderful figure amid loud cheers. Then and then only was her dream realized, her work done, her prayer answered.

The opera house or town hall on North Main street was erected in 1878 at a cost of sixteen thousand dollars. In 1890 it was remodeled at a cost of three thousand dollars. In all it has cost the town about twenty thousand dollars. It contains besides the opera house, the mayor's office, armory and prison cells. Although this is a somewhat pretentious building yet it is in many respects poorly arranged and inadequate. The town needs and will soon have in the near future a modern assembly hall suitable to its needs.

NEWSPAPERS. ·

Mechanicsburg has THE NEWS ITEM, published weekly, and THE MORNING TELEGRAM, issued daily.

The News-Item, then called the "REVIEW" was first published in 1869, Ezekiel Mettles, editor and proprietor. In 1871 O. C. Wheeler took charge, changing the name to The Mechanicsburg News. In 1876 John Church bought it. When he retired W. H. Baxter became proprietor. Then O. C. Wheeler returned and started an opposition paper called The Mechanicsburg Herald. In 1883 Jones and Brown consolidated them as The Mechanicsburg Screw-driver. It was then purchased by

William Morris and Howard Mannington who rechristened it The Mechanicsburg News. Morris and Walker then published it until 1898, then Morris and Slater until 1903. O. E. Shaw also published a paper called The Item from 1893 to 1903 when Shaw and Hulmes purchased the NEWS and consolidated the two papers under the present title, The Mechanicsburg News Item. This paper now has a circulation (1917) of fifteen hundred copies and goes all over the United States, and even reaches Canada.

In 1903 Charles C. Slater began the publication of our first daily, The Morning Telegram, published and delivered at the door every morning at 6:30. It has a circulation of 500 copies. Its principal purpose is the quick dissemination of local news.

RAILROADS.

Our one railroad is now a part of the Big Four system and is operated as a short line between Springfield and Delaware. As it is twenty-three miles shorter than the route through Columbus, it is used mainly for through freight. There are but two passenger trains each way daily. The local patronage is considerable, the receipts yearly for passenger fares are $10,800, and for freight $54,000. There are 450 cars of live stock shipped yearly from this station. The local freight business is quite considerable.

TELEPHONE.

The telephone exchange is on the corner of Main and East Sandusky streets, D. J. Burnham, president, and H. Clay Rogers, secretary and manager, and employs fourteen people. This exchange had 25 subscribers in 1898 but has at the present time one thousand or more.

GAS WORKS.

In 1878 A. L. McCabe built the Gas Works as a private enterprise putting V. S. Magruder in charge. Thomas Needham was employed as operator. In 1881 the plant was destroyed by fire. In order that the town might not be deprived of the use of gas a stock company of 1,800 shares was formed among the citizens to purchase and restore the works. Mr. John C. Sceva is the president. V. G. Riddle has been the efficient operator all the time from then to the present, 36 years.

CHAPTER 16.
Lodges and Societies.

THE various secret orders and societies are entitled to great commendation for their share in creating a better Mechanicsburg. At first the idea of their being secret caused much suspicion if not discredit in the minds of many, some churches forbidding membership to any one who belonged to a secret order. In later years these lodges were given their proper standing in the community.

MASONS.

The charter for the Clinton Lodge No. 113 Free and Accepted Masons was granted in 1843. The first Worshipful Master was Dr. Obed Horr. The first petitioners for membership were D. F. Spain and David L. Tullis. They met in various halls until their first assembly room was built over the M. P. Church in 1855. This becoming untenable through the cracking of the walls was sold to the church for $500 in 1889. The name was changed from Clinton to Mechanicsburg lodge. They met in rooms fitted up over the Central Bank until 1909 when the present handsome and commodious Masonic Temple was erected on Main street. It is a fine ornament to the town. It contains a basement club room; a reception room, banquet hall and kitchen on the first floor; a reception and lodge room on the second. The membership in 1917 is 215.

There is also a chapter of Royal Arch Masons (Mechanicsburg R. A. M. No. 168) of 80 members. The charter was granted in 1899 and it has made a slow but constant growth since its organization. The masonic bonds of brotherhood and helpfulness are very close. Their friendship is very apparent when needed most. It is a most ancient and honored order.

THE EASTERN STAR.

The Caroline Chapter of Eastern Star, a masonic auxiliary, eligible to masons, their wives, mothers, daughters, sisters and widows, was organized here in 1894 with 36 charter members. They now have 109 members who are very loyal and interested. Their object is the uplifting of humanity, and their teachings are constancy, fidelity, purity, hope of immortality and love.

ODD FELLOWS.

The Wildey Lodge of Odd Fellows was organized here in 1855. William H. Palmer, D. F. Spain, Lewis Kingsley, Morgan Baldwin, R. B. Rogers, Gilbert Farrington and John C. Price were the charter members. As far as can be ascertained the lodge met in rented rooms until 1870 when the three story brick block was erected on the corner of the square. At present the Odd Fellows own the north half of the building, their lodge room being in the third story, and dining room in the second The membership is 125 of the substantial men of the community. The constitution of the order provides obligatory assistance to the sick and disabled and also payment of the funeral expenses. After this if the family of the deceased is in need they are helped from what is called the Charity fund. The ritual is founded on the benevolent teachings of the Bible.

The Rebekaks, the woman's auxiliary organization numbers fifty.

The colored Odd Fellows lodge, organized in 1881, occupies the old Baptist church on Locust street. The number of members at present is 25. The woman's auxiliary order of Ruth numbers 20.

KNIGHTS OF PYTHIAS.

The Homer Lodge of Knights of Pythias named for Homer Porterfield of Indianapolis, a former resident, was organized in 1891. In 1894 their castle on Main street was built. This structure and all of its contents: beautiful paintings, rugs, and paraphernalia was destroyed by fire in 1916. Their membership has grown from 35 to over 160 virile young men who are making themselves felt in the community. It is a very remarkable fact that in its short history here it has lost by death, removals and discontinuances 123 members. This order being founded on the classical story of Damon and Pythias must of necessity emphasize brotherhood and chivalrous ideals.

The Pythian Sisterhood was established in 1907 and now numbers about 50.

RED MEN.

A lodge of the Independent Order of Red Men was established here in the year 1874 with a charter membership of 14 braves. The roll is now 47. During the Revolutionary war there was a secret society called "Sons of Liberty" founded on the Indian idea. The company which threw the tea overboard in Boston Harbor was disguised as Indians. The Red Men's Order of today is a continuation of the order of the "Sons of Liberty." It is now a beneficiary order.

MODERN WOODMEN.

The Lodge of Modern Woodmen was organized here as late as 1900. J. A. Whitehead was the first chief executive. There were only 15 members at the start. This has rapidly increased until it numbers 103. The order is organized on the insurance plan, based on purely financial principles.

THE GOSHEN FARMERS' INSURANCE ASSOCIATION.

The Goshen Farmers' Insurance Association has grown from $136,000 worth of property insured in 1895 to $1,270,000 at the present time. During the 22 years of its experience it has paid $51,883 in losses. John Hodge was its first president. Mr. A. L. Mumma the originator and organizer of the company has been the secretary and manager since its organization. This company has been honestly and wisely managed. Mechanicsburg is justly proud of her insurance company. The territory in which it operates includes Champaign, Clark, Madison and Union counties.

MACCABEES.

The organization of the Maccabees Tent No. 496 was effected here in 1911 with fifteen members. R. A. Venrick is the Commander, W. F. Hendricks the record keeper. The Tent has now 35 members. Insurance is paid by this order on sickness, accident, or death. It is an exclusive organization for mutual insurance. The organization once owned $10,000 of our school bonds. The State of Ohio has 40,000 Maccabees, and the United States 350,000.

THE GRANGE.

The Advance Grange has grown since its organization in 1912 from 50 to 250 members, of men and women interested in agriculture, whether living in town or on the farm. While the Grange has not found all that it started out to do to be practical, especially the establishment of Grange stores, yet it has found a place of great usefulness in the furtherance of agricultural interests.

GRAND ARMY.

Stephen Baxter Post of the Grand Army of the Republic was organized in 1878. Starting with over a hundred soldiers and sailors of the civil war, its ranks have crumbled until but 34 of the gray-haired veterans remain. William H. Boulton is the present Commander. Each year on the thirtieth of May their ranks become thinner and their step less firm as they march in the parade to decorate their dead comrades' graves with flags and flowers. White haired old men they are. Soon, right soon, we will yearly decorate their graves too.

THE KING'S DAUGHTERS.

A circle of King's Daughters was organized here in 1897 by Mrs. Fannie Ott, consisting of her Sunday School Class. From that has grown the Earnest Workers Circle of 40 members and the Sunshine Circle of 26 members. These are united in what is called "the city union." Their motto is help to any one in need. They have just furnished a rest room on Sandusky street in the Hotel buliding.

W. C. T. U.

The Woman's Christian Temperance Union grew out of what was called the "Woman's Crusade" of 1873 which was a thorough try out of the power of moral suasion to abolish the liquor traffic, also a prayer test asking and expecting God to do for us what we as American citizens would not do for ourselves. The women would march from an all day prayer meeting at the church to the places where intoxicating beverages were sold and kneeling on the dirty floor or muddy street would pray as suffering women only can pray, and sing religious songs This effort as all other kindred efforts such as the Washingtonian, The Knights Templar, The Blue Ribbon Movement, failed of permanent results, except the organization of the Woman's Christian Temperance Union which is still having a far-reaching influence for the suppression of the liquor traffic by law.

WOMAN'S TOURIST CLUB

by its interest in the public welfare has become a prominent factor in our city life. It was organized in 1894. It now numbers 65. Fifty are active members and 15 associate. It meets semi-monthly and its object is to develop fellowship among women and promote the best practical methods of self-improvement.

THE BOY SCOUTS

were organized in the present troop on January 15, 1914. H. Clay Rogers was appointed Scout Master, Superintendent Bert Highlands, Assistant Scout Master and Prof. Welsheimer, Assistant. Upon the removal from town of the last named, Thomas Erwin was elected Assistant Scout Master in October of the year of organization and these three have continued in office to the present time. There are now three patrols with an enrollment of 29. They have had a scout hall fitted up for two years where they hold regular meetings once a week. One room is fitted up with a work bench and tools of all kinds. They have held three very successful, well organized camping trips. True to their object, the scouts of our town are being built up in character and good citizenship.

THE CAMP FIRE GIRLS

were organized about two and a half years ago with a membership of 19, with an advisory board from the Woman's Tourist Club. Miss Alice Robinson was first guardian for a short term. Mrs. C. S. Amidon was the second, and Mrs. Elijah Horr is the present guardian. Their object is to develop the home spirit, to organize a girl's daily home life that the daily drudgery may be made to contribute to the beauty of living, and to promote happy social life.

THE WOMAN'S RELIEF CORPS,

an auxiliary to the G. A. R., was organized here in 1887 with 35 charter members. Mrs. Tully McKinney and Mrs. John E. Davis, assisted by Mr. John Culbertson were instrumental in forming the organization. Mrs. Pollyann Guy was the first president. There are now 52 members and Mrs. John Van-Ness is president. Their object is to honor and assist old soldiers and sailors and their families in various ways.

SONS OF VETERANS.

A camp of the S. of V. was mustered in by Captain W. F. Hendricks in 1909 with 35 members. Mr. Bruce Neer was first

Commander and Capt. Hendricks, first secretary and mustering in officer. During their existence 65 have been mustered in, and at present there are about 30 in good standing. The worthy object of this organization is to do honor and service to the veterans of the civil war.

CHAPTER 17.
Mechanicsburg in 1917.

ENTERPRISES.
STANDARD OIL COMPANY.

FARTHEST east on the railway and at the end of Mill street are the yards of the Standard Oil Company from which coal oil and gasoline are distributed by two tank wagons to the adjacent territory. The plant consists of two buildings and four tanks.

THE WING SEED COMPANY

is one of our most important enterprises, doing an annual retail business aggregating one hundred and fifty thousand dollars in farm, garden and flower seeds and bulbs. This company lays claim to having the finest collection of peony, dahlia and iris bulbs west of the Alleghenies, having in all some 500 varieties.

Like all successful enterprises the business started in a small way by the late Joseph E. Wing furnishing to farmers the purest and best alfalfa seed at cost. From this benevolent beginning, under the management of Charles B. Wing, has grown the great, widely known, "Wing Seed House." Their motto has been and is, "Always the best." The plant is along the railroad east of the depot.

THE SHIPPING PENS

and stock scales are just west of Wing Seed House.

THE SISSON & ROBINSON LUMBER YARD

is on the railroad at the intersection of Locust street with extensive and most modernly arranged buildings for handling lumber, coal, brick, cement, and all kinds of roofing. Their immense stock of lumber is shipped in already planed, contrary to the old custom, because it is found the reduction in freight more than pays the cost of planing.

THE FARMERS' ELEVATOR

adjoins them on the west. They handle all kinds of grain and coal. They sell a good self-feeder for stock which is the invention of their manager, Mr. O. H. Clough.

THE BURNHAM & HYDE

feeding and sales barn and yard are just south of the elevator. They have excellent facilities for handling horses, cattle, sheep and hogs for sales and shipping purposes.

THE BROWN ELEVATOR

has a most advantageous situation on Main street at its intersection with the Big Four railroad. It was formerly the Hunter elevator. It has a large and increasing trade in wheat, corn, oats, clover and a variety of grass seeds, all kinds of feed, salt, tankage, etc. Coarse grinding and cleaning seed is done.

THE LONG MILL AND ELEVATOR

is farther south on Main street. The old Staley Mill before mentioned still stands as a part of their plant, although greatly improved and enlarged. The Long company put in up-to-date machinery. The justly celebrated "Ohio Home Flour" is manufactured here. Here is the electric light plant and an ice plant. They also deal in coal. The business is greatly facilitated by a private railroad switch.

WEAVER & BOWEN

are next, occupying a building built on a part of the foundation of the burned drill factory with a farm supply store. They handle windmills, fencing, roofing, pumps, gasoline engines, furnaces and a variety of things.

DANIEL MC CLARENS

coal, brick, cement and sewer pipe yard we find by returning to Locust street, near the railroad. He also manufactures cement blocks and other cement products.

CLEMANS & ALEXANDER

have their hardwood lumber yard and sawmill a little north on Locust street. Most of their sawing is commercial lumber, although custom sawing is done.

THE HOME DAIRY, ICE AND ICE CREAM FACTORY

is farther north on Locust street. Their new modern building, 50 x 95 feet is supplied with the best appliances. Their capacity is 8 tons of ice per day. There is also a storage room for 90 tons. A great saving is made by using the same brine which freezes the ice to freeze the ice cream. Auto trucks are used for gathering the cream from the farms and also supplying them with ice and ice cream. Nearby villages are also taken into the routes. They have an abundant supply of deep driven well water which rises to the top and is so abundant that an engine pumping constantly can only succeed in lowering it six inches. Harold Hopkins is the energetic local manager.

CULBERTSON BROTHERS

have their carriage and automobile shops on the corner of Locust and East Sandusky streets. Farther towards Main street is their extensive garage and repair rooms. They are exclusive agents for the Ford, Hudson and Jeffery cars and have large sales.

THE CHINESE LAUNDRY

is next door west. Mr. Hong Lee returns to China every ten years to visit his family which consists of a wife, a daughter and two sons. He has been in the laundry business 40 years.

BURNHAM & HYDE

have purchased this laundry building and will remodel and build it into offices for their stock exchange, with barns and yards in the rear.

It is thought the old Burnham livery barn loafers' club will occupy rooms here. Their By-laws provide for a fine of a dime against any member or guest who uses an oath or tells an obscene story, and the proceeds from the fines to be invested in peanuts and other refreshments for the club.

HUNTER'S IMPLEMENT WAREHOUSE

is the next building. It is large and filled to overflowing with a variety of farm machinery.

J. D. STEWART'S GARAGE

improved and refitted is the Burnham brick livery barn. Elevators and the most modern appliances have been put it. They are agents for the Chalmers and Elcar automobiles, also make a specialty of farm tractors and other implements. Their sales are large.

THE HANLEY-MADDEX COMPANY.

has a large clothing store on the southeast corner of the public square. Besides all kinds of men's furnishings they sell hats, boots and shoes and ladies' shoes. They have been in business for 18 years, having succeeded Bien Brothers. Their sales are some twenty-five thousand dollars per year.

W. H. HUNTER'S HARDWARE

and implement store is next on down the east side of South Main street. The father, John Hunter, with William Osborn conducted it 25 years. It has been under the present management for 20 years. It carries an immense stock and is one of the old, solid enterprises of the town.

H. N. GILBERT'S

gents' furnishing store is next. He carries a large stock of clothing, hats and shoes. Mr. Gilbert has conducted this business for 16 years. His aim is quality. With his customary pertinacity he will soon rebuild his store three doors below which was destroyed by fire.

THE R. B. BYERS

dry goods store, successors to G. C. Newman company has a fine location. Besides dry goods they keep an elegant line of wall papers, rugs and furnishings.

V. S. MAGRUDER & SON,

after passing the burned district we cross the alley to the entrance of the upstairs offices of this firm. Mr. Magruder is the successor to E. D. Morgan in the insurance business. He began in 1867, Mr. Magruder taking charge in 1900. The business has grown to such proportions that three people are kept constantly busy. They represent twelve strong companies.

THE STURGIS MEAT MARKET

and delicatessen shop is on the first floor of the Magruder building. Mr. Sturgis is successor to Mr. Joseph Metzner who was in business in this location for 16 years.

P. T. MOORE'S DRY GOODS.

Fifty-nine years ago young Jesse Moore began clerking in a dry goods store. Being methodical and as regular as a clock he could always be found today at the same place he was yesterday. He was either at the store or had gone home to his meal. This steadiness with a little more enterprise was inherited by his son, P. T. Moore, who has continued for nine years to make this store a success. His motto is "aim to keep the best at what it is worth." He sells dry goods, rugs and carpets.

THE PRINCESS THEATER

for moving pictures has been brought to a high standard by Mr. Ernest J. Maugans, the proprietor. He aims to give his patrons the best films and his shows are equal to the city productions. He is most generous in giving benefits for charitable purposes.

RICHTER'S RESTAURANT

below the Princess serves either a lunch or fine meal at all hours of the day.

LONGBRAKE AND REECE'S

store is an exclusive Family Shoe Store. They are deserving young men and by fair and courteous treatment expect to win. They carry a large stock and draw trade from a wide territory.

LEGG & OSBORN

Thomas Morgan learned the tinner's trade of James Riddle. Being of a business turn in an early day he started a hardware store and tin shop which he continued until 1893 when Mr. Weed bought it and conducted it for two years. Stewart and

Legge had it until 1901, Sivey & Hull until 1904, Hulmes & Legge until 1912. Legge & Osborn (J. P. Legge and Clifford Osborn) have conducted it for the last seven years, so there has been a hardware store in that place for more than 50 years. Besides an ample stock of general hardware and stoves, they keep harness, roofing and fencing.

THE BUCHWALTER & ADAMS

general merchandise emporium including dry goods, groceries, wall paper, carpets, rugs, boots and shoes. Their terms are strictly cash. From a small start the business has grown to large proportions.

THE FARMERS' BANK

was established in 1865. It is in great contrast to its predecessor, "The Mechanicsburg Bank" started by Richard D. Williams as a private bank, with twenty-five thousand dollars capital. Thomas Davis was cashier. In 1884 it was incorporated as The Farmers' bank, with a capital stock of $100,000. It has $44,000 surplus and undivided profits. It is a United States and Ohio State Depository. It is called "the old reliable". In its long history it has had but three presidents, R. D. Williams, Dr. J. H. Clark and J. C. Sceva, the present incumbent. It has had but two cashiers, Thomas Davis and F. M. Clemans.

GRIFFIN'S BARBER SHOP

is just south of the above bank. It formerly belonged to John Yocum. This tonsorial parlor is modern in all of its appointments.

THE AMERICAN EXPRESS COMPANY

has an accommodating agent in Mr. Ed. Vought. Mrs. Vought is also in the employ of the company. Mr. Vought reports that the business here is far above that of other towns of its size, the recent receipts averaging around thirteen hundred dollars per month. The income is greatly increased by the shipping of The Wing Seed Company.

EARL PARSON'S SHOE REPAIR SHOP.

Upon entering this shop you will miss the old time cobbler's bench with knife, hammer and awl, and will find the best up-to-date machinery run by electricity. The earnings, mostly for repairs, were fourteen hundred dollars last year. The business has grown from twenty dollars to an average of $150 per month.

LAURA BAKER'S MILLINERY

store has been conducted in the same place for a number of years and she has given good satisfaction to her customers. She carries a big line of women's and children's ready to wear hats, and does a good business in trimming.

A BLACKSMITH SHOP

has been conducted just below the millinery for more than forty years, now by Ed. Conway.

MR. CHARLES LEAVITT

is a dealer in poultry, eggs, vegetables, fruit and honey. His apiary two miles above town yielded six tons of honey last year.

CALLAHAN'S

grocery is a square south of the above line of business houses, on the corner of Main and Oak streets. He deals also in vegetables and fruits.

SNELL DAVIS

will conduct an automobile repair shop where the Stewart garage has been for a number of years.

FRANK LOCKE'S HOTEL

and restaurant is the last place of business above the railroad on the east side of Main street.

THE HALLEY GROCERY STORE

is opposite the Locke hotel on the west side of Main street.

DR. H. C. DICKSON'S OFFICE

is about a square north of the railroad. He is the very efficient and careful Health Officer for the corporation.

JOE BUNCHES' BARBER SHOP

is exclusively for colored men.

BROWN'S RESTAURANT

is well patronized by our colored population. They enjoy it as a convenient social center.

L. A. FREEMAN & CO'S

automobile tire, repair and vulcanizing trade is increasing as excellent work is done. This is a new store.

HESS' GROCERY

and meat market handles staple groveries, fresh fruits and vegetables, fresh and cured meats. Mr. Hess is not connected with the central delivery system, but delivers promptly by auto truck.

HUPP & SON.

Major George Hupp began the business of cabinet making and undertaking early in the history of the town. O. C. Hupp, his son, took charge of the business in 1882. It is now conducted by O. C. and Walter E. Hupp as "Hupp & Son". Besides keeping a large assortment of furniture, they make undertaking a specialty. They conducted 16 funerals the first year they were in business and they now have from seventy to eighty per year. They have a fine auto hearse and ambulance, and also keep a horse-drawn funeral car for those who prefer it.

FRED OWEN'S BOOKSTORE

has been operated by him since 1889. It is the only bookstore and queensware store in town. Mr. Owen has a double store room, one section is stocked with all kinds of queensware, and the other with books, stationery, toys, notions. etc. His sales are large and he has been quite successful.

OUR POSTOFFICE

has been promoted to a second class office. This is partly due to the output of the Wing Seed Company. Last year $8,000 worth of stamps were sold and the amount is increasing. The periodicals received here show that we have a reading people. There are four rural routes out of town driven by Harry Wood, W. B. Owen, Tyler Bradford, and Ben Mahoy.

C. L. MC CORKLE

has been in the harness business for 48 years. He learned the trade in the "Dad" Magruder shop. He has associated with him in the manufacture and repair of harness, his son, Lew McCorkle. Starting without a cent of capital they have built up a big business. They also sell whips, robes, trunks and traveling bags.

CHARLES A. WOOD

is an attorney of high standing and has also been a Justice of the Peace for twenty years. By referring to his carefully kept docket he reported that the last entry was Number 553, and that there had been an equal number settled before being entered. Who would suppose that there were over a thousand justice cases during his tenure of office, or fifty such cases a year. Mr. Wood is representative of a good line of insurance companies.

THE CENTRAL BANK

is one of the strongest banks in the county. Its solidity consists in the personal liability of its stockholders who own 8,500 acres of land which is held for the liabilities of the bank. Its assets amount to one million dollars, and its stock is now valued at five hundred dollars a share. It was organized in 1890 with Chandler Mitchel as president. P. J. Burnham has been its cashier for 27 years, ever since its organization. Calvin R. Hunter succeeded Mr. Mitchel as president.

LEHNE'S JEWELRY

store is in the south half of the Taylor Block. Mr. Adolph Lehne succeeded Robert Embrey about twenty years ago. The outfit at that time consisted of a workbench, a few watches to be repaired and one small case of jewelry. Under Mr. Lehne's management this has grown to a fine jewelry store that is equal in its appointments to any in the city. He carries a heavy stock and handles Edisons, Victrolas and pianos.

CHARLES KELLER'S PHARMACY

which occupies the north side of the Taylor building, is up-to-date in all of its appointments and in its management. Everything is kept here which constitutes a first class drug store, drugs,

medicines, toilet articles, candies, cigars, etc. They are sales-
men for the Rexall products.

DR. E. R. STOCKWELL, THE VETERINARIAN,

has his barn and offices on the outlot in the rear of Lot No. 12,
back of Keller's drug store. With the facilities furnished by
the automobile his practice extends over a wide radius. His
business has been very successful.

STOCKWELL & MITCHELL

are agents for the Buick automobile. Their office is in the same
building with Dr. Stockwell's office.

THE BIDDLE STUDIO

successors to Bess Colwell's Photograph Gallery, is centrally
located. The entrance is just below the Central Bank.

BOULTON & WARE'S BUILDING

is across the alley from the Taylor building. On this historic
spot the first clearing in town was made and a log cabin built, used
as a storeroom and bank. This was in 1814. Boulton & Ware
carry a very heavy stock of groceries, fruits, vegetables, hay and
feed.

THOMAS B. WARE, ATTORNEY,

has a suite of offices on the second floor of the above-mentioned
building. He has been engaged in the practice of law since
1901 . He is secretary and attorney of the Mutual Loan & Savings Company, Township Clerk, and Registrar.

He is a member of the law firm, Owen, Ware & Owen, with
offices here and in Urbana.

F. E. GANNON'S

modern and up-to-date grocery was founded in 1903. Mr. Gannon keeps his store in good order and is an expert in the display
in his line: groceries, fruits and vegetables.

CHARLES FULLERTON, TAILOR,

occupies the second floor of the Gannon building. He does fine
work and has a big trade.

H. H. SHAW'S PHARMACY.

Harold Shaw is successor to Daniel Ernest who was in the drug business many years. His stock of drugs, toilet articles, hospital supplies, box candies and cigars is complete. He has two elegant soda fountains and has built and furnished a beautiful palm garden for the comfort of his patrons.

JOHN LEIDY'S CONFECTIONERY.

Mr. Leidy began his business career in this town thirty-five years ago, starting with a small bakery. Now in his own building, with the assistance of Mrs. Leidy he conducts a large confectionery and bakery with a fine soda fountain and ice cream parlors.

MRS. MAE HELMER'S MILLINERY STORE

is in the south end of the hotel building. She has been in business for fourteen years. She carries a large stock and her store is first-class in every way. She tries to please by selling only good goods at reasonable prices.

ANDERSON INN.

We come now to another historic spot, the southwest corner of the public square. Here the first log tavern was erected in 1815 by Warret Owen. These days are more fully described in a former chapter. It is a remarkable fact that here and here only has a tavern or hotel flourished in 102 years of the history of Mechanicsburg. The ANDERSON INN, as it is now called, is a three story brick building with basement. Mr. Charles Hanley has lately purchased it from Dayton parties and is repairing and refitting it with modern conveniences. The present efficient manager, Mrs. Elmer Anderson, will continue for at least three years.

L. F. STROUP'S VARIETY STORE

is on the northeast corner of the square in the Odd Fellows' block. He carries a complete line of notions of every description and is very accommodating in securing whatever his customers want.

THE NEWS-ITEM OFFICE

is on the second floor of the Odd Fellows' building. All kinds of job work are done here besides the publication of a weekly paper.

THE RED MEN

have their lodge rooms on the third floor of this building.

FLOYD JOBE'S BAKERY,

confectionery and ice cream parlors are in the north rooms of the Odd Fellows' building, while his new modern bakery is on East Sandusky street. Fine baking is his specialty.

W. W. OSBORN'S INSURANCE OFFICES

are on the second floor above the Jobe Bakery. Mr. Osborn has some of the best companies and is courteous and fair in the adjustment of losses. He insures against fire, tornado, accident, and writes life and automobile insurance.

ODD FELLOWS' HALL

is on the third floor. A history of their organization is given in a former chapter.

JOHN BRINNON'S MEAT MARKET

is in the old Traders' Bank building, and was established in 1901. He keeps the best of everything in his line, and is most accommodating in his dealings.

DR. O. A. NINCEHELSER

takes precedence in town in length of practice, having looked after the health of this community for thirty years. During the first six years he was in partnership with Dr. J. H. Clark.

THE INGMAN MERCHANT TAILORING SHOP

has been in the business for forty years. Some of the best citizens are its patrons. It is now conducted by E. W. Ingman.

DAVIS & BYERS

(T. J. Davis and E. L. Byers) carry a very large stock of furniture and draw trade from a wide territory. They also have a modern undertaking establishment, with auto hearse and ambulance, and a horse drawn hearse if any one's preference is expressed for it. According to the report of our two undertaking establishments, there is an average of three funerals a week in this supposedly healthy place, but of course this includes a wide country territory.

DR. J. C. HATHAWAY

has a brick office building next to the Davis & Byers store. He has a large practice to which he gives close attention.

ALBERT KOLB'S SECONDHAND STORE

is on the north side of East Sandusky street in the building known as the Cottage Hotel. He is also a dealer in poultry and eggs.

HARRY H. DARLING'S BLACKSMITH SHOP

stands just across the alley. Mr. Darling has been in the business for 41 years and in the present location for 37 years. He learned the trade from Wm. Yeasell and formerly had his brother, Charles, associated with him.

JAMES WAUGH'S BARBER SHOP

is next on the west. Here most excellent work is done. He has the patronage of many well-pleased customers.

POOL ROOM AND RESTAURANT

On the northeast corner of the square is a poolroom which changes proprietors with the changes of the moon.

TELEPHONE EXCHANGE.

On the second floor of this brick building on the square is the exchange and the offices of the manager, H. C. Rogers. The growth of their business has been described elsewhere.

THE CALVIN ARMFIELD TONSORIAL PARLORS

with bath room and shoe shine accommodations is the first store on the east side of Main street, going north. Mr. Armfield has been in business 41 years and has large patronage.

MRS. BROWN'S MILLINERY

is in the brick building formerly occupied as offices by Dr. Demand. Although the last milliner to enter the business, Mrs. Brown has a good trade.

THE VENRICK TIN SHOP

is in one of the .oldest buildings in town. It was known in an early day as the Owen & Keyes drug store. They are expert tinners and repairers.

THE MASONIC TEMPLE

is the handsome building next. It has been described before.

C. W. MARTIN'S GROCERY

keeps a good, clean, up-to-date stock. It is called, "the home of good eats".

THE TOWN HALL

or Opera House has been described elsewhere. In the rear is the fire engine house with a suite of rooms on the second floor for the driver.

DR. W. A. STOUTENBOROUGH

has offices and residence just north of the town hall.

DR. H. O. OGDEN

is located with offices and residence on the south side of West Sandusky street.

DR. L. E. BAKER

has offices and residence on the north side of West Sandusky street.

DR. E. H. THORPE, DENTIST,

is also located on West Sandusky street, three doors from Main street. His large practice is well cared for.

MINISTERS.

There are four resident ministers at present, Methodist Episcopal, Methodist Protestant, and two colored, Methodist and Baptist.

WELL DRIVERS.

There are two well drivers, T. E. Burnham and George Darling.

GEORGE SEWELL

has a general repair shop on East Mill street. He can repair or make anything desired in fine workmanship.

SAMUEL ROBINSON & SON, BLACKSMITHS

and wagon makers have their shop on South Main street, just beyond the corporation line.

G. C. CLEMON'S GROCERY

is on the edge of town in one of our suburbs, Nashville.

STOCKDEALERS.

Our stock buyers are Burnham & Hyde, B. H. Moody, and Bailey & Saxbe.

THE CEMENT GRAVE VAULT FACTORY

is in the rear of the Davis & Byers store. Owing to the weight of the vaults the cost of freight curtails their use except at nearby points. Where used they are largely taking the place of stone. The proprietors are T. J. Davis and John Reece.

TRAINING BARNS AND RACE TRACK

on the Matinee Park grounds are convenient in every way for breaking colts and training racers. A number of fast steppers have been developed here.

THE CHARLES JACK FLORAL AND VEGETABLE GREENHOUSES

are on the extreme end of West Sandusky street and furnish employment to six men. Mr. Jack assists on the trial grounds of the Wing Seed Company.

WILLIAM ROBERTSON'S CLEANING

establishment is on Oak street near the depot. All kinds of fabrics are cleaned by machinery at reasonable prices, rugs are made and dyed and an electric house cleaner is operated.

THE GREENVILLE GRAVEL COMPANY

located west of town employs from 30 to 50 men. Their annual output of washed gravel, sand and crushed stone was last year 9,312 carloads. Next year with the night shift it will probably be 1500 cars. The immense machinery is run by electricity.

The bed from which the gravel is taken is forty acres in extent and has a perpendicular face of 30 feet.

PLUMBERS.

V. G. Riddle & Son and T. E. Burnham are our plumbers.

THE MUTUAL LOAN & SAVINGS CO.,

organized in 1889 has been a great help to the town in a business way, and has been the means of securing homes for people who could not otherwise secure them and has been a savings bank for many people. J. J. Culbertson is president, having succeeded Dr. C. E. Demand last year. The capital stock has now increased to $600,000. This is one of our best and most helpful enterprises.

THE MODEL BARBER SHOP

Ladies Hair Shampooing and Face Massaging a Specialty

Prices Reasonable.

Toilet Water, Creams and Hair Tonic for Sale.

We Aim to Please.　　　　　　　W. F. GRIFFIN, Prop.

CHAS. A. WOOD

ATTORNEY-AT-LAW _____ 1884
JUSTICE OF PEACE_____ 1897
INSURANCE _____ 1895
MAYOR _____1900, 1900

C. L. McCORKLE

Dealer in and Manufacturer of

Harness, Saddles, Bridles

BLANKETS, ROBES, WHIPS, TRUNKS, ETC. REPAIRING A SPECIALTY.

JOBE'S

BAKERY AND CONFECTIONERY

Phone No. 12.　　　　　　　　　　NORTH MAIN ST.

AA5207R

CPSIA information can be obtained
at www.ICGtesting.com
Printed in the USA
BVHW03*1720161018
530215BV00004B/501/P

9 781169 023611